LITERACY ASSESSMENT

A Collection of Articles
From the Australian Literacy
Educators' Association

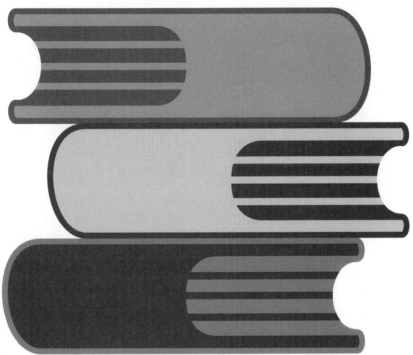

HEATHER FEHRING

Royal Melbourne Institute of Technology University
Bundoora, Victoria, Australia

Editor

INTERNATIONAL
Reading Association
800 Barksdale Road, PO Box 8139
Newark, Delaware 19714-8139, USA
www.reading.org

The International Reading Association attempts, through its publications, to provide a forum for a wide spectrum of opinions on reading. This policy permits divergent viewpoints without implying the endorsement of the Association.

Director of Publications   Joan M. Irwin
Editorial Director, Books and Special Projects   Matthew W. Baker
Production Editor   Shannon Benner
Permissions Editor   Janet S. Parrack
Acquisitions and Communications Coordinator   Corinne M. Mooney
Associate Editor, Books and Special Projects   Sara J. Murphy
Assistant Editor   Charlene M. Nichols
Administrative Assistant   Michele Jester
Senior Editorial Assistant   Tyanna L. Collins
Production Department Manager   Iona Sauscermen
Supervisor, Electronic Publishing   Anette Schütz
Senior Electronic Publishing Specialist   Cheryl J. Strum
Electronic Publishing Specialist   R. Lynn Harrison
Proofreader   Elizabeth C. Hunt

Project Editors   Shannon Benner and Janet S. Parrack

Cover   Design and Illustration, Linda Steere

Permissions
Requests to reprint or photocopy individual articles should be sent to the Australian Literacy Educators' Association. See http://www.alea.edu.au for contact information.

Library of Congress Cataloging-in-Publication Data
Literacy assessment : a collection of articles from the Australian
  Literacy Educators' Association / Heather Fehring, editor.
       p. cm.
Articles were originally published between 1992 and 2002.
Includes bibliographical references.
  ISBN 0-87207-004-2
1. Language arts—Ability testing—Australia.   2. Reading—Ability testing--Australia.
3. Literacy—Australia—Evaluation.   I. Fehring,
Heather. II. Australian Literacy Educators' Association.
  LB1576.L5564 2003
  428'.007'1--dc21

2002154828

CONTENTS

EDITOR

Heather Fehring
Associate Professor in Literacy Assessment
Faculty of Education, Language and Community Services
Royal Melbourne Institute of Technology University
Bundoora, Victoria, Australia

AUTHORS

Nola Alloway
Associate Professor
School of Education
James Cook University
Townsville, Queensland, Australia

Lynne Badger
Senior Lecturer
Faculty of Education
University of South Australia
Adelaide, South Australia

Brian Cambourne
Associate Professor
University of Wollongong
Wollongong, New South Wales,
    Australia

Jenni Connor
Senior Policy Officer
Tasmanian Department of
    Education
Hobart, Tasmania, Australia

Melissa Dash
Teacher
Killara Primary School
North Sunshine, Victoria, Australia

John Davidson
Teacher
Spensley Street Primary School
Clifton Hill, Victoria, Australia

Ros Fryar
Teacher
Mansfield Primary School
Reynella, South Australia

Pam Gilbert
Professor of Education
School of Education
James Cook University
Townsville, Queensland, Australia
(Pam Gilbert died in November
    2002)

Greer Johnson
Senior Lecturer
School of Cognition, Language &
    Special Education
Griffith University
Nathan, Queensland, Australia

Kaye Lowe
Visiting Professor
University of Kentucky
Lexington, Kentucky, USA

Michael McNamara
Assistant Principal
Craigieburn Secondary College
Craigieburn, Victoria, Australia

Marion Meiers
Senior Research Fellow
Australian Council for Educational
    Research
Camberwell, Victoria, Australia

Kate Mount
Teacher
Northern Territory, Australia

Anne Nelson
Assistant Principal
Spensley Street Primary School
Clifton Hill, Victoria, Australia

Robyn Perkins
Teacher
Kensington Primary School
Kensington, Victoria, Australia

Christina E. van Kraayenoord
Senior Lecturer
Schonell Special Education
    Research Centre
Graduate School of Education
The University of Queensland,
    St. Lucia
Brisbane, Queensland, Australia

Lyn Wilkinson
Lecturer
School of Education
The Flinders University of South
    Australia
Adelaide, South Australia

Jeff Wilson
Teacher
Moonee Ponds West Primary
    School
Moonee Ponds, Victoria, Australia

Lorraine Wilson
Educational Consultant
Carlton, Victoria, Australia

Claire M. Wyatt-Smith
Associate Professor
Faculty of Education
Mt. Gravatt Campus
Griffith University
Nathan, Queensland, Australia

Introduction

In the last 10 years, encompassing the end of the 20th century and the beginning of the 21st century, the world has witnessed a massive change to the nature of what it means to be literate. The "Information Age" of the new millennium is a world where global and multicultural education, internationalization of the curriculum, and the notion of multiliteracies exist. In this world of new learning it is no longer feasible to speak of literacy as if it were a unitary concept. Learners in the Information Age must access, understand, transform, and transmit information at an exponential rate:

> *Accessing* information requires identifying and finding printed, oral, and graphic information; *gaining* information requires comprehension, analysis, synthesis, and evaluation; *transforming* information requires writing, speaking, and representing; and *transmitting* information means publishing or disseminating transformed knowledge. (Kibby, 2000, p. 380)

Educators in the 21st century must address very challenging questions:

- What does it mean to be literate in the 21st century?
- How can we effectively assess students' literacies?
- How can we ensure that the assessment process empowers an individual?

It is no longer meaningful to assess literacy as if one measure is appropriate for all interested stakeholders. There are many voices to consider in any process of literacy assessment and reporting. These voices require different information to address their needs. Educators must consider the following:

- the needs of the **students**—what do students want and need to know about their own learning achievements?
- the rights of the **parent(s)**—what is our responsibility as educators to parents concerning their children's achievements?
- the professional **responsibility to colleagues**—how much and what information should be passed on from one professional to another?
- the **accountability** demands of governmental systems—what information needs to be gathered regarding student achievement to justify the financial outlay to taxpayers?

- the **macropolitical agenda**—what is the macropolitical agenda influencing assessment and reporting practices?

Teachers in Australia, like our colleagues in the United States (Afflerbach, 2002), are weighed down by a testing regime that is driving the federal, political, educational environment.

The voices of these stakeholders are interconnected and interrelated. They place many demands on teachers in terms of the professional knowledge required to make efficient and effective judgements and the time required to plan and coordinate such decision-making processes. Teachers need to collect a range of information in order to make informed, consistent, and balanced judgements regarding students' literacy achievements. The use of one-off, single-testing instruments is not appropriate. Building a portfolio (Fehring & Wilson, 1996) of a student's work from a range of multimodal and multidimensional assessment techniques provides the rich data from which teachers can build a profile of a student's literacy competence.

The authors in this collection of articles present a diversity of viewpoints related to literacy assessment and reporting. The collection consists of 19 previously published articles from the following Australian Literacy Educators' Association (ALEA) publications:

- *The Australian Journal of Language and Literacy*—a journal that meets the needs of both classroom teachers and academics by providing clear links between theory, research, and practice
- *Literacy Learning: The Middle Years* (previously titled *Literacy Learning: Secondary Thoughts*)—a journal primarily for secondary teachers who wish to develop students' literacy and learning competencies across the curriculum
- *Practically Primary*—a journal with practical, informative ideas for primary classroom teachers
- ALEA National Conference papers

The articles were selected on the basis of the following criteria:

- The articles were published between 1992 and 2002.
- Some articles explicate different principles of literacy assessment from a theoretical perspective.
- Some articles report literacy-assessment research studies.
- Some articles tackle standards and benchmarking issues.
- Some articles demonstrate the practical classroom implementation of literacy and reporting techniques.

- The articles encompass a range of schooling from primary (elementary) to secondary (high school).
- All articles address the importance of teacher judgement in relation to the assessment and reporting of students' literacy.

The collection is organized around wide-ranging themes of teacher judgement (article 1); information technology (article 2); self-assessment (articles 3–5); cultural diversity issues (articles 6 and 7); portfolio techniques (articles 8–11); literacy assessment in the post–primary (post–elementary) sector (articles 12–14); and issues related to the testing, benchmarking, and standards debate (articles 15–19). The articles are as follows:

Fehring, H. (1998). Understanding the influences on teachers' judgements in the process of assessing and reporting students' literacy in the classroom.
> This article reports on a research study examining the influences on teachers' judgements of students' literacy development within three primary school environments in Victoria, Australia. The study concludes that the most powerful and enduring change in the classroom will be achieved by professionally informed, reflective, and articulate teachers.

Mount, K. (1997). Assessing information literacy: A reception class learns the skills and how to assess their learning.
> This article outlines a functional suggestion that combines curriculum content and assessment in one process. Concentrating on information literacy skills and using an observational checklist, the author has created a very practical technique with children in their first year of schooling. This idea could be adapted and replicated in any teaching environment.

Fryar, R. (1997). Students assess their own reporting and presentation skills.
> This article on self-assessment techniques with Year 6 and 7 students is full of practical suggestions. The author has combined information about the research process with both speaking and listening outcomes and writing outcomes. This results in a valuable self-assessment checklist for upper primary classroom teachers and students. Empowering students at all levels of the educational spectrum is essential if we want reflective, analytical, and independent learners. This article should be read in conjunction with the following article by Robyn Perkins.

Perkins, R. (1999). Children's self evaluations.
> The author has made a compilation of children's own reflective self-evaluations. The comments by the children speak for themselves as to the value of involving students in the assessment process.

van Kraayenoord, C.E. (1994). Toward self-assessment of literacy learning.
This article focuses on the connection between self-assessment, self-reflection, and metacognitive abilities, a triad that is critical in the development of independent learners. The author reminds readers that if we value multidimensional literacy learning, this needs to be encompassed in assessment programs, not just as a narrow subset of measurable items. The article describes an array of self-assessment techniques that can be used through the portfolio strategy: reading and writing logs; checklists, questionnaires, and inventories; student–teacher conferences; collaborative writing; and peer and personal share-time activities. The section on frequently asked questions about the self-assessment strategy is an extremely useful resource for students, teachers, and parents.

Badger, L., & Wilkinson, L. (1998). Literacy assessment of students from poor and diverse communities: Changing the programs, changing the outcomes.
This article is about the challenges faced by teachers working in disadvantaged primary schools and grappling with literacy assessment and equity issues. This research-based project explores the classroom reality of socially and culturally loaded assessment and literacy programs. One aim of the research was to document what makes a difference for students in disadvantaged schools. The authors document how equitable literacy outcomes are facilitated by breadth and diversity of literacy practices in schools.

Connor, J. (2002). Assessment: Profiling literacy with young Indigenous children.
This article reports on a project that developed a preschool profile for Australian Indigenous children. The author highlights the necessity of taking into consideration issues of cultural diversity and inclusivity when designing assessment practices.

Wilson, L., & Dash, M. (1999). Using running records in the classroom.
The authors remind us that the real value of running records is to "provide teachers with information about the child's use of the cuing systems—graphophonic, syntactic, and semantic."

Nelson, A. (1999). Authentic assessment and system accountability.
The author illustrates how she combines a number of valuable literacy assessment techniques to gather rich information about the reading progress of children in her classroom. By combining strategies such as running records, teacher observations, student self-assessment, and cross-age tutoring, the author is able to address both the official reporting requirements and the students' parents' needs.

Davidson, J. (1999). All things in moderation: A whole school approach to authentic assessment.

> The author writes about a whole school approach to the management of the assessment process, referring to the use of a "Cumulative File" of students' work. *Portfolio assessment* is a widely used alternative term for this approach. How to manage effective and efficient assessment and reporting practices is a question constantly asked by all educators. The author addresses some of the key issues in this article. This article complements the following article by Jeff Wilson.

Wilson, J. (1999). Portfolios: Valuing the whole of children's learning.

> The author writes about the use of portfolios, which he defines as "a collection of children's work that shows significant aspects of development throughout the year." A key challenge for all teachers is what to collect, when, where, and why as evidence of a student's progress. The author gives a number of valuable classroom-based examples of assessment techniques used in the school where he teaches.

Johnson, G. (1998). Making the invisible visible: The language of assessment tasks.

> This article highlights the important relationship between critical literacy and literacy assessment. To be critically literate in the Information Age of the 21st century will be even more important than ever before. However, empowering students to become critically literate needs to involve explicit instruction and discussion not only about the reading process, but also about what is to be assessed and why. The author documents a case study of one teacher and his Year 11 English class exploring a text and using an assessment technique involving critical literacy attributes.

McNamara, M. (1992). Reading assessment options for teachers of junior secondary students.

> This work deals with reading assessment in Year 7 and 8 classrooms. The article includes an in-depth analysis of a Year 8 student's retelling of a text. The author deconstructs for the reader the attributes of the student's knowledge of the text from the retelling process. In so doing, he demonstrates how the criteria used to make the assessment are evidenced in the student's reading and retelling. The major theme underpinning this article is that the purpose of the assessment process should determine the techniques chosen to collect the decision-making data. The work centers on three broad purposes of assessment:

1. assessment for curriculum (knowledge about individual student's abilities),

2. assessment for communication (assessment for certification purposes), and

3. assessment for accountability (assessment for the political purposes of system decision making).

The article also highlights the fact that whatever reading-assessment technique is used, educators need to remember that each is founded on a particular view of the reading process. The theoretical constructs underpinning the assessment technique determine what is chosen as important to be tested and how each component is tested. When selecting a reading-assessment technique, it is important to know what you are assessing and why.

Lowe, K. (2000). Graded self assessment.
This article reminds us of the key criteria for success when dealing with self-assessment in senior classes. The article is based on the author's observations of a senior English classroom in Virginia, USA, and draws together a number of issues such as

- respect for the learner;

- trust in the process, which involves explicit knowledge of the assessment criteriap; and

- integration of learning and assessment practices into holistic curriculum.

Incorporated in this article is a description of three assessment techniques: literature letters (lit letters), reading logs, and class participation. This article is a powerful reminder of the necessity to empower students to understand their own learning.

Cambourne, B. (1992). Testing times for literacy?
This article is a timely reminder that effective and efficient literacy assessment will not be found in the simplistic and narrow measurement model of statewide or national testing. This is not, and will never be, the answer to the literacy needs of students, teachers, and parents.

Cambourne, B. (1999). What's the score on testing?
This second contribution by Brian Cambourne reminds educators of the need to keep in perspective the shortcomings of large-scale testing programs. If our objective as educators in the assessment of students' literacy is to provide information that will assist all stakeholders to

facilitate learning, we must seek multidimensional and multimodal techniques.

Wyatt-Smith, C.M. (2000). Exploring the relationship between large-scale literacy testing programs and classroom-based assessment: A focus on teachers' accounts.

This provocative article uncovers another aspect of system, large-scale testing programs that is rarely reported in the bureaucratic summaries of the testing results. "What is clear is the need for systems to improve their performance in communicating to teachers information about national and state policy initiatives in literacy testing and how these relate to curriculum and pedagogy." The article makes clear that teachers are committed to formative assessment, whereas the system is interested in summative testing programs.

Alloway, N., & Gilbert, P. (1998). Reading literacy test data: Benchmarking success?

This article exposes the politics of literacy assessment. The article challenges the reader to understand the creation of the myth of "crisis" in literacy education by large-scale testing programs. The authors critically analyse what is reported as literacy achievement versus what is actually tested. Large-scale testing programs historically test only what is measurable by a "paper and pencil" writing test. This study also examines the issues of gender and socioeconomic inequalities in the testing results. The article raises the issue of the total inadequacy of these tests in a world where children are operating in the new Information Age driven by information technology. The authors offer insightful, important questions about not only the values implicitly part of large-scale testing programs, but also school practices that will enhance socioeconomic equality and change.

Meiers, M. (1996). Assessment, reporting and accountability in English and literacy education: Finding the signposts to the future.

This paper was a keynote address given at the 22nd National Conference of ALEA. This article has been included in this collection because, although it is historical in its perspective and very Australian in its orientation, it mirrors many of the issues confronted by U.S. educators in the last decade. The theme of this work, as the title states, is assessment, reporting, and accountability. These three aspects of literacy assessment do not always sit comfortably together. The author's work is an extensive coverage of the interrelationship between such issues as the following:

- The public face of literacy assessment as portrayed in the media—a face that does not always reflect the reality of a complex process.
- The needs of the diverse range of stakeholders involved in student assessment (the students themselves, parents, general tax payers who fund public education, and politicians who are often more interested in the rhetoric than the reality).

The summative conclusion highlights the need for balance and diversity in a literacy-assessment program.

This collection provides a rich source of different perspectives covering a wide range of topics. However, all articles highlight the importance of teacher judgement as being fundamental to efficient and effective literacy-assessment and reporting practices in the classroom. Professionally informed teachers who are articulate, knowledgeable, and reflective practitioners are the change agents of the future:

> The most powerful and enduring change in the classroom will be achieved by professionally informed and articulate teachers. Teacher judgement needs to reflect such expertise, because it is the teacher who is one of the most instrumental links between the minds of students and their future achievements in the multiliteracies required in the 21st century. Collaboration involving the diversity of voices seeking reform in literacies is essential. Meeting the literacy expectations of the 21st century will be achieved, not by a battle, but by an orchestrated and integrated alliance. (Fehring, 1999, p. 274)

—Heather Fehring

REFERENCES

Afflerbach, P. (2002). The road to folly and redemption: Perspectives on the legitimacy of high-stakes testing. *Reading Research Quarterly, 37*, 348–360.

Fehring, H. (1999). *Influences on teachers' judgements of students' literacy development in a Victorian context.* Unpublished doctorate of philosophy thesis, RMIT University, Melbourne, Victoria, Australia.

Fehring, H., & Wilson, J. (1996). Practical portfolios: Assessment and evaluation in the primary classroom. *Practically Primary, 1*(2), 16–19.

Kibby, M.W. (2000). What will be the demands of literacy in the workplace in the next millennium? *Reading Research Quarterly, 35*, 380–381.

Understanding the influences on teachers' judgements in the process of assessing and reporting students' literacy in the classroom

Heather Fehring

The most powerful and enduring change in the classroom will be achieved by professionally informed and articulate teachers. It is the teacher who is one of the most instrumental links between the minds of students and their future achievements in the multiliteracies required in the 21st century. Collaboration involving the diversity of voices seeking reform in literacies is essential. Meeting the literacy expectations of the 21st century will be achieved, not by a battle, but by an orchestrated and integrated alliance.

The research reported in this paper examines the influences on teachers' judgements of students' literacy development within three primary school settings in Victoria, Australia. The research provides documentation of the explicit and implicit influences on the decision-making processes of three teachers regarding their literacy judgements. The three case-study sites are located in metropolitan Melbourne in Victoria.

The study in context

If teachers base their practices upon their beliefs at any given point in time, then they need to recognise how their beliefs influence decisions about what and how they teach. Documenting such influences is an important step in understanding the judgement-making process and in turn improving such processes. By documenting teachers' articulation of the influences, the research highlights the complexity of the decision-making process.

It is timely to do this research—the massive technological changes that are occurring in the communication networks are challenging us to reconceptualise our notions of literacies and practice. Adapting to the complex

From *Literacy for All. Conference proceedings of the Joint National Conference ALEA & AATE*, July 1998.
Reprinted with permission of the Australian Literacy Educators' Association.

interconnections created by the hypertext of technological writing, reading, and thinking will change our teaching and learning strategies. However, is such development possibly putting in jeopardy the human–interaction component, historically considered essential in the cognitive development of young students? In the foreword to *Evaluating Literacy: A Perspective For Change* (1991), Garth Boomer wrote:

> Australian teachers for literacy must fight to retain both their preeminence and their rights as the best judges of how well their students are doing. Any schemes that are devised for national reporting on literacy achievements must be grounded in and informed by the rich judgments of the teachers who see children at work every day. (Anthony, Johnson, Mickelson, & Preece, 1991)

The research process in this study took a constructivist, interpretive approach and interpreted through description and analysis. The pivotal focus of the study was around the experiences of three teachers, Alexandra, Georgina, and Victoria (pseudonyms). The research sites comprised three schools located within metropolitan Melbourne. Qualitative methods of data collection were the main sources of information in this study. Ethnographic techniques such as on–site field observations, both participant and non–participant observation, interviews involving the three teachers and key informants, content analysis of school curriculum documents, and artifacts were the main sources of data. This methodology was chosen because there is a need to increase naturalistic research in the field. There is a need to have the case rich descriptions of teachers articulating just what does influence their decisions if the profession is to improve.

> One major implication of our failure to understand and assist teachers with the task demands of classroom assessment may be the extensive use of unsound measurement procedures in our schools. The result of poor measurement is poor decision making. At the very least, poor decisions mean inefficient instruction, and at worst they can lead to failure to learn.... (Stiggins & Conklin, 1992)

The data analysis process was managed using two computer programmes. In 1990, seven key themes emerged to explain the influences on teachers' judgements of students' literacy development.

Major findings

The major findings of this study are interpreted as spheres of influence. Seven major spheres emerged to describe the influences on teachers' judgements of students' literacy development, and each major sphere consisted of several distinguishable features. The teacher is situated at the centre, as it is the teacher's point of view that is reflected in the diagram. The significance of the influences on each individual varies. Figure 1 is a diagrammatical representation of the interconnected themes that represent the major spheres of influence.

The major spheres of influence are summarised in Table 1.

Conclusions related to the major findings

The seven major spheres of influence indicated by the data in this research study are encapsulated in two dimensions of interacting relationships. There is a powerful intrapersonal dimension unique to each of the participating teachers in this study. In addition, there is an ecology of context dimension

Figure 1. Diagrammatical representation of the spheres of influence on teachers' judgements of students' literacy development

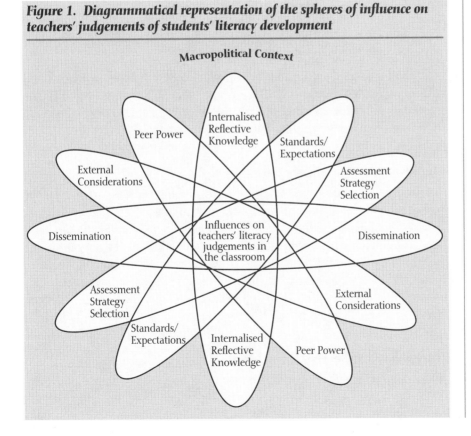

Understanding the influences on teachers' judgements in the process of assessing and reporting students' literacy in the classroom

11

> **Table 1. Influences on teachers' judgements of students' literacy development that emerged from the current research study**
>
> • **Internalised Reflective Knowledge:** a complex integration of experience, tacit knowledge/intuition, common sense, accumulated knowledge, professional competence; and an underlying theoretical philosophy of language learning that the individuals use as a conceptual base for their assessment practices.
>
> • **Assessment Strategy Selection:** specific assessment strategies used to gather data selected on the basis of philosophical compatibility, cost efficiency, and time effectiveness.
>
> • **External Considerations:** external professional considerations related to the influence that experts and professional development programmes have had on teachers' thinking; how teachers respond to Department of Education Victoria (DoE) policy directives; the impact of individual school policies and curriculum documents on classroom practices and the significance of school charters on teachers' work routines.
>
> • **Dissemination:** the reporting of literacy achievement to the educational community.
>
> • **Peer Power:** the impact of significant peers upon individual teachers and the power of the leadership demonstrated by school principals.
>
> • **Standards/Expectations:** the expectations underlying literacy standards and the judgement criteria determining such standards.
>
> • **Macropolitical Context:** the changing macropolitical context and the ramifications of policy changes at both the state and federal level.

that encompasses the external influences upon the teacher's judgemental decision-making processes. The ecology of context dimension refers to the integration of influences that occurs in the teachers' immediate surroundings. The following section contains a presentation of the conclusions.

The intrapersonal dimension

The intrapersonal dimension encompasses the themes that are within the cognitive domain of each individual, such as the internalised reflective knowledge of each individual built up from experiential interaction in educational environments; the intricate interplay of tacit knowledge or intuition, teacher judgement and professional knowledge; and the articulatory practices that require teachers to explicate their professional judgements, reconstructing them into spoken language. The elements of the intrapersonal dimension are discussed in the next section.

Internalised reflective knowledge

Internalised reflective knowledge emerged as a powerful influence on teachers' judgements of students' literacy development. The significance of the classifications of this influence was that the elements were a complex integration of features unique to each participant, although common patterns emerged across participants and these patterns may be common to other teachers. The patterns that emerged were related to each participant's knowledge of the field of literacy assessment. A comment by Victoria, in relation to a discussion we had about her student-evaluation book, highlights the essence of this influence: "...it makes me realise that when I look at it I have so much in here [pointing to her head] which I am sure is true of many teachers" (K.10.3).[1] The reality of internal reflective thinking is demonstrated when teachers articulate their knowledge. The power of this influence lay in the internalised theoretical principles of language learning that the teachers embraced. The label "internalised reflective knowledge" emerged as it became important to distinguish it from the concepts of "tacit knowledge" and "intuition."

The literature review identified a number of writers who describe tacit knowledge as an important component of teachers' judgement-making ability (Cambourne & Turbill, 1994; Elbaz, 1981; Hargreaves, 1977; Shulman, 1987). The unconscious and implicit nature of tacit knowledge has meant that it has not been investigated in relation to its component elements. However, the research in this study has revealed an influence on teachers' judgemental processes that is identifiable by a complex integration and interplay of features that are internal to the individual but can be articulated and identified as teacher knowledge. Although such features are internalised, when teachers were encouraged to discuss their literacy assessment procedures and beliefs, they were able to articulate many of the features of this influence on their judgement-making processes. There were two fundamental properties to all three teachers' internalised reflective knowledge: the defining qualities of their concept of literacies and the philosophical theory of literacy learning that underpinned the teachers' curriculum planning. These two considerations were building blocks on which the teachers based their judgemental decisions.

The conceptualization of literacy: A basic building block

Alexandra, Georgina, and Victoria's judgemental processes are closely tied to their articulated concept of literacy. All three teachers in this study define literacy as a complex integration of speaking, listening, reading, writing, viewing, and critical thinking skills. Alexandra has a more unitary concept of literacy using the terms reading, writing, speaking, and listening. Georgina includes viewing, thinking, and the notions of critical analysis, communication, and the importance of across curriculum literacies as ongoing processes. Victoria's concept of literacy encompasses "the ability to be able to speak clearly, to listen to and understand what someone else is saying, and to be

Understanding the influences on teachers' judgements in the process of assessing and reporting students' literacy in the classroom

13

able to appraise what is said." She emphasises comprehension, writing, and being able to write for many purposes, viewing, and critical analysis. However, Victoria adds the comment: "but I feel that the written word is a bigger basis for literacy in primary schools" (ITQ–PB–Q1).[2]

All three teachers articulate what is currently a most popular 1990s usage of the literacy concept. In addition, it is noteworthy that in the document called *Literacy for All: The Challenge for Australian Schools* (Department of Employment, Education, Training and Youth Affairs, 1998), which is the 1998 Commonwealth Literacy Policies for Australian Schools, the following definition is acknowledged as the widely used definition of literacy in Australia in recent years. "Effective literacy is intrinsically purposeful, flexible, and dynamic and involves the integration of speaking, listening and critical thinking with reading and writing (DEET, 1991, p. 5)" (DEET, 1998, p. 7).

The teachers' assessment practices reflect their understanding of what constitutes literacy. As acknowledged by Alexandra, Georgina, and Victoria, computer literacy and viewing as components of the literacy concept are very recent additions to the debate regarding literacy. The notion of multiple literacies, a phenomenon written about extensively in the 1990s (Gee, 1991; Lankshear, Gee, Knobel, & Searle, 1997; Luke & Gilbert, 1993; The New London Group, 1996), is not explicitly referred to by participants in this study. However, it is important to note that the teachers in this study work within a context focused on school literacy. School literacy is a sub-set of multiple literacies and needs to be understood and investigated in this light.

Alexandra very strongly defended her position that integrated learning, inquiry-based curriculum, and the importance of context to children's learning influenced her decision of how to assess. Both Georgina and Victoria hold equally strong beliefs that their assessment practices must reflect their beliefs about what is literacy and how children learn. Accordingly, they plan teaching and learning programmes that incorporate experiences facilitating the development of these components of literacy. Consequently, they also plan assessment and reporting strategies that cover the range of literacy attributes within such a definition and in what have been commonly referred to as authentic contexts. The close tie between integrated curriculum and literacy-learning activities reported by the teachers illustrates this connection. The literacy assessment strategies chosen by Alexandra, Georgina, and Victoria reflect formative practices, criterion-based achievement, and descriptive reporting procedures.

In the literature reviewed for this study it was not uncommon to find writers describing literacy as an integration of many facets of language learning. However, when they report achievements in literacy they report the results of a reading or writing test. The popular media are involved in this practice as well. Many headlines and articles can be found in the press, reporting so-called literacy standards. However, they are in many cases articles regarding the results of single reading tests. The substantial works of Green et al. (1994a, 1994b, 1997) document much of this history of the reporting of literacy standards. This issue of the controversy over what is termed literacies and what is tested and measured has been commented on for many decades and was so clearly articulated over 20 years ago in the British report *A Language for Life*.

Theoretical models of language learning: A second building block

The three case-study teachers articulated strong philosophical beliefs in models of English language learning emanating from the psychocognitive era (1970s and 1980s). More specifically, the theoretical stance taken by all three case-study teachers reflects the view published under the label of the psycholinguistic process of language acquisition. Under this umbrella is the whole language approach to the teaching and learning of the English language. The teachers' views reflected this approach. Cross-checking the teachers' beliefs with the stated beliefs in the respective school policy documents illustrated common underlying philosophies. Triangulating the data of the literacy-assessment strategies used in the classrooms of the three teachers with literacy-assessment strategies researched in the literature as encompassing psycholinguistic principles also produced a common picture. There was an internal consistency amongst the articulated beliefs of the teachers, the stated school policy documents, the teaching and learning activities observed during the observation sessions, and the analysis of the interview data.

However, one inconsistency was observed in the interview data and the school policy documents: the teachers' articulated beliefs that reflected a knowledge of the genre school of literacy acquisition. The "genre school" is commonly ascribed to the socio-cultural era of the late 1980s. This era encompasses the systematic functional grammar of Halliday, the genre school, the influence of the critical theorists, and the emergent influence in the 1990s of multiple literacies. When cross-checking the teachers' beliefs with the policy documents of the schools, no substantial reference could be identified in the documents to the theoretical base of the teachers' views. It would seem that the teachers' knowledge base was reflecting, and they were incorporating into their daily teaching practices, theoretical beliefs from the socio-cultural understanding of literacy acquisitions and literacy learning. The policy documents of the respective schools had not been rewritten to incorporate such changes. Some curriculum documents dated back several years and the school charter documents work on a three-year cycle. There was a developmental time lag between the teachers' classroom practices and the official documentation of the schools' curriculum policies. The interesting situation was that the three teachers were changing their classroom practices to incorporate the 1990s philosophy that had emanated from the genre school of theorists based at Sydney University (Australia). However, teachers do not have the luxury of the academic world. The academic world is able to hypothesise and advocate change with regard to the teaching and assessment of literacy free from the shackles of bureaucracy. Teachers must work within the concept of a "school literacy" that encompasses quite different groups of educational stakeholders. The power and expectations of these influential groups have also been demonstrated in this research study. The influence identified as "macropolitical context" illustrates just one of the influences that impinge on teachers' decision making.

Another interesting feature, in relation to the influence of the teachers' underlying theoretical principles upon their literacy judgements, is the situation that has arisen in Victoria with the Learning Assessment Project (LAP) testing programme. The state-wide testing programme is based on different theoretical literacy and learning principles to the language and learning and assessment philosophies of the teachers and of the curriculum policies of the case-study schools in this research. Many Victorian teachers have refused to be involved in the LAP testing programme. In the initial testing years there had been industrial action in opposition to the LAP. The three case-study schools in this research did not support the LAP. However, the teachers have been directed by the DoE to administer the LAP tests to children in Year 3 and Year 5. The reality of the classroom is such that central directives override the theoretical principles and philosophies of the teachers. This situation once again demonstrates how the powerful influence of the macropolitical context impinges upon the assessment and reporting practices undertaken at the individual school, teacher, and student levels.

The effects of articulation on teachers' internalised reflective knowledge

Another interesting observation arose from this study. An issue related to participants articulating their beliefs emerged during the ongoing analysis of the interview data. The iterative process involved interviewing study participants, reading curriculum documents, talking to key informants, and making observations in the classroom context. This process resulted in cross questioning, revisiting discussions from one session to another, and checking information in documents with discussions with participants. As a result of this intense and extended interaction, comments began to emerge that indicated the participants were rethinking, clarifying, and analysing their positions on various issues as a result of articulating their beliefs in discussion. The very act of conversing with another person about their views was activating a reflective process that was enhancing the teachers' own understanding. For example:

- In one of the interviews with Alexandra we were discussing what assessment techniques she used in conjunction with specified standards references and the following comment was made: "Because I was thinking about what you were saying, there are four main things..." (K.2.30)
- In relation to how Alexandra analyses a cloze exercise she commented: "Yeah, yeah, you don't reflect on why you do these things until you are asked." (K.3.13)

The act of making explicit what was perhaps considered tacit knowledge encouraged the teachers to reconstruct their knowledge and raised their own self-awareness. This phenomenon may be linked to the influence called personal receptivity, the notion that an effective teacher must be receptive to the influence of change. Are the teachers who can openly articulate their internalised reflective knowledge the teachers who are not threatened by the challenge of change? This question would be an interesting study in its own right. Alexandra, Georgina, and Victoria were able to discuss their beliefs, defend their teaching and learning philosophies, adapt their understanding of multiple literacies to take on board computer literacy, and incorporate the teaching of genre in their curriculum. These three teachers were not threatened by change but embraced new developments in literacies.

It became apparent that the ongoing interactive questioning between the participants and myself was in actuality developing the reflective process. The notion of teachers' voice was a fundamental component of the research methodology in this study. Therefore, the research process relied heavily on discussing and interacting with the teachers, asking the teachers questions, seeking clarification from document analysis, reiterating my observations of the daily classroom practices for feedback from participants, and critically analysing actions and belief statements of participants. The very practices of discussing, questioning, and asking the teachers to reflect and articulate their beliefs were facilitatory processes in the clarification of the teachers' literacy-assessment ideas. Both Alexandra and Victoria commented on the influence that talking to me was having on their thinking

Understanding the influences
on teachers' judgements
in the process of assessing and
reporting students' literacy
in the classroom
17

about the issues involved in making judgements about students' literacy assessment. In one conversation regarding what constitutes literacy Alexandra commented that she had been watching a TV show about literacy after our initial discussion. I commented, "That's highly commendable. So I've got you thinking about this, have I, Alexandra?" (L.4.3). Alexandra replied, "Well you have. I can't think of anything else, everywhere I go I hear oh literacy! What is it today?" (K.4.3.). These snippets highlight the significance of reflection in the following situations:

- the importance of colleagues talking,

- the impact of professionals discussing literacy related items, and

- the power of personal interaction when a researcher takes an interest in another teacher's literacy practices.

In addition, the issue of having a conducive environment, the time and opportunity for discursive reflection is highlighted by this observation. Such a situation has ramifications for both moderation processes and professional development activities at the school, system, and tertiary training level.

The results of this research highlight the powerful impact that professional development has on teachers' knowledge of literacy acquisition, language-learning process, and assessment and reporting practices. The phenomenon that emerged from the observations in this study relates to the significance of teachers articulating their beliefs, philosophies, and teaching and learning strategies. Professional development that uses the transmission model of experts imparting their knowledge to participants may not be capitalising on maximum learning. Teachers articulating their ways of knowing and their beliefs about literacy practices may well prove to be a more effective technique for developing internalized reflective knowledge. Hill and Crevola (1997) recently commented:

> Arguably the most important element in any design aimed at improved teaching and learning in school is the provision of effective, ongoing, professional learning opportunities for teachers related to their classroom practice. Such opportunities extend well beyond traditional forms of professional development and in-service training to include observation and mentoring. (p. 10)

The current research extends this notion of professional development further. Internalised reflective knowledge is enhanced through the process of teachers articulating their principles of teaching and learning and of literacy-assessment practices. Hill and Crevola (1997) state: "effective teachers make a habit of monitoring and assessing their students' progress" (p. 9). However, the process involves more than just undertaking the assessment. The teachers in this study not only know why they use certain assessment techniques, but they are also able to articulate what the results of the assessment process mean and what they will do as a consequence of the judgements they have made. This connection between reflection, articulation, and action needs to be a fundamental part of the professional development process.

Literacy assessment and reporting strategies

The teachers' selection of literacy-assessment techniques was another powerful influence on their judgement-making process. The teachers in this study selected literacy-assessment strategies that reflected the philosophical stance they believed in regarding literacy acquisition. There was clear congruence between the techniques and the teachers' beliefs in formative assessment. There were no assessment techniques of a summative nature chosen by the teachers. The only summative tests used by the teachers were either imposed on them by external authorities (for example, the LAP testing programme), or were practice scholarship examinations to prepare Year 6 students for the transition tests they would be required to sit if they chose private secondary schooling.

The assessment-strategy observation was nominated by all three teachers as being an important technique for the collection of literacy data. This finding complements other recent Australian work (Dilena & van Kraayenoord, 1996a, 1996b; Forster & Masters, 1996; Masters & Forster, 1996; Moni, Tonkin, & van Kraayenoord, 1996). However, further elaboration of issues involved in observation needs to be researched in depth. When teachers report that they use observation as an assessment technique, what behaviours are observed? Why is a particular behaviour chosen for observation? What reference criteria do teachers use to comparatively evaluate the observation? To strengthen not only the power of the technique of observation, but also the teachers' ability to articulate the use of the strategy, further studies in this area would be very valuable. Research of this nature would no doubt provide a wealth of information to inform both preservice teachers training and post-initial professional development programmes. In 1991 a comprehensive report entitled *Teaching English literacy: A project of national significance on the preservice preparation of teachers for teaching English literacy* (Christie, 1991, August) was published. This project investigated the education and training needs of teachers across Australia. The results of this study overwhelmingly documented the need for teacher training courses to increase the studies devoted to English language and literacy.

Understanding the influences
on teachers' judgements
in the process of assessing and
reporting students' literacy
in the classroom
19

Recommendation 8: That over a four year period of study, student teachers should complete a program 20 per cent: (or about six semester units) of which is devoted to language and literacy studies. (Christie, 1991)

The fact that student teachers across the nation had fewer than six units of study in English language and literacy studies is a damning criticism of teacher training. The report also comments on the lack of English language and literacy studies that include issues related to literacy assessment. Further research in the area of teacher judgement and literacy assessment could make a valuable input into the courses training institutions offer future teachers.

When examining the influence of the selection of assessment strategies a finding emerged that was based on a group of elements labeled as "contextualised." This feature was distinguished by classroom organisational considerations. Key selection criteria of literacy-assessment strategies were based on whether the techniques were:

- Too expensive in monetary terms. Some assessment techniques were not selected because of the prohibitive cost of the items. There were literacy-assessment techniques nominated as being of practical use to the teacher. However, due to the monetary cost of the item teachers could not buy them within their English language curriculum budget allocations.

- Too costly in terms of a teacher's time to administer. "Running records" and "miscue analysis" were named as assessment techniques that the teachers believed they did not have enough time to administer on a regular basis.

- Inaccessible in terms of difficulty to organise. The example given by Georgina was the use of parent interviews as an assessment technique; the difficulty of arranging such interviews prohibited frequent use of this data–gathering method, so it was in effect inaccessible literacy–assessment data.

- Based on a belief that the evidence gathered and the judgements made on the basis of such data were justifiable. The notion that a teacher's judgements must be credible in the eyes of the students was a determining feature of the assessment techniques selected.

What have emerged as influential factors regarding the teachers' selection of assessment techniques are the criteria that the strategy must be philosophically compatible to the literacy-learning theory held by the teachers, and a group of elements that run counter to theory and are based on very practical organisational considerations. In some cases the theoretical criteria are overruled by the cost and organisational difficulty of administering some assessment techniques.

This discovery has significant ramifications for school and system allocation of funds. Literacy-assessment strategies that are theoretically consistent with the curriculum philosophy and appear beneficial for teachers to use are not being used by teachers because the techniques are too expensive and too time consuming to organise. The possible inadequacy of funding at the school level may be restricting the implementation of effective assessment practices. In addition, the organisational structure of schools and classrooms needs to be reexamined. Alexandra and Georgina both commented that they could not use certain techniques because the curriculum is so crowded that there is not enough time in the day to allocate more time to specific assessment techniques. This research clearly indicates that there is no simple linear relationship between the philosophy of the curriculum and assessment, and the techniques chosen to assist teachers to make literacy judgements. The data from Alexandra, Georgina, and Victoria are testament to this situation. New research investigating this phenomenon across year levels, between classroom teachers and curriculum specialists, and amongst novice and experienced teachers may shed more light on the phenomenon and provide recommendations for change.

The ecological dimension

The ecological dimension encompasses a teacher's working environment. It relates to the spheres of influence on teachers' judgements of workplace factors. Micropolitical webs within the school such as school councils, principal directives, significant peers, and policy and curriculum programme documents influenced teachers' judgements. Macropolitical influences relate to government directives at both the state and federal levels and to funding issues that directly impinge upon the decision-making process of a teacher in the classroom. These spheres are complex networks of influence that produce the educational environment in which teachers must work. In comparison to the intrapersonal dimension that operates within the individual teacher's internalised decision-making processes, the ecological dimension provides the web often outside the teachers' control. The major elements of the ecological dimension are summarised in the next section.

External consideration

The teachers in this study were all influenced by situations external to their personal judgemental processes. This cluster of influences was an intriguing collection. Some external influences had been accommodated into the

Understanding the influences on teachers' judgements in the process of assessing and reporting students' literacy in the classroom

21

teachers' decision-making processes, as for example the schools' curriculum policies; some influences had been directly imposed upon the teachers who had little choice but to comply, as for example the CSF and the LAP; and some influences had been taken on board because of the credibility of the acknowledged expertise of the programme or person. This situation raises a number of pertinent considerations. How effective is compulsion when related to changing teachers' practices? What are the consequences of enforced directives on classroom curriculum across year levels? What are the consequences of enforced directives on teachers, students, and parents? How do acknowledged experts influence teachers' thinking and classroom practices? What are the distinguishing attributes of an influential expert? These questions provide the basis for many future studies.

The influence of significant others on teachers' judgement-making processes

The findings of this research indicate that the teachers involved considered the opinions and instructions of a range of significant peers. The participants acknowledged that the principal's power was twofold; first, the power vested in the principal as a consequence of the authority of the position; secondly, the principal viewed as a curriculum leader in her/his own right. The teachers perceived that the principal influenced their judgements by recognised expertise and by direction or compulsion. This finding has ramifications for principal leadership training in management courses.

The influence labeled "significant peers" was also an interesting diverse collection of attributes. Peers could just share information with other peers as in collegiate working relationships or role-model situations. Peers could be internal mentors who appeared to be qualitatively more influential as they were recognised for their expertise and curriculum leadership qualities. In conjunction with this finding is the related effect of moderation upon teachers' judgemental processes. Moderation in the three case-study schools in this research was considered to be more informal than a formally adopted process. However, moderation was viewed as an important process in collegiate sharing of knowledge. This finding complements the results of the comprehensive project entitled *Whole School Approaches to Assessing and Reporting Literacy* (Dilena & van Kraayenord, 1995, 1996a, 1996b). "Teachers, for example, value collaborative reflection as a means for deepening and broadening their knowledge about literacy issues and value the expertise of their colleagues" (Dilena & van Kraayenord, 1996a, p. 36).

These findings together have important ramifications for both system and school-level professional development planning. If professional development programmes are to have maximum effect on the implementation of new conceptualisations of multiple literacies and change within systems organisation and school curriculum, the power of significant peers needs to be taken into consideration. Further research needs to investigate the parameters and powers of significant peers, asking questions such as:

- Who are the powerful peers in a school context?
- How do peers influence each other?
- In what contexts are peers a powerful influence on each other?
- What are the attributes of an influential peer?

Research in these areas would provide valuable knowledge for the structure of mentoring and post-initial professional development programmes.

Dissemination of literacy achievement information

The reporting of students' literacy achievements is a vexed issue. Alexandra, Georgina, and Victoria are influenced by their concern in the following areas:

- to report with integrity regarding their philosophical beliefs about literacy learning and literacy achievement,
- to maintain credibility with the students by reporting their literacy strengths and weaknesses in an equitable and justifiable manner,
- to communicate to a varied audience of parents in an informative fashion, and
- to provide accountability requirements demanded of them by the DoE Victoria.

These influences often conflict with each other. The teachers sometimes had to choose between reporting in terms of descriptive criterion-based outcomes that were linked to the curriculum of the classroom, school and individual student's achievements, and reporting relating to arbitrarily established achievement benchmarks. The ideological dilemma for these three teachers stemmed from their strong theoretical beliefs in many aspects of the whole language approach to literacy learning.

The issue of standards or the influence of external reference criteria

To be able to make an evaluative judgement about a student's literacy development, a teacher needs a reference criterion. For example,

- an expected standard or benchmark,
- a developmental learning continuum, or
- a hierarchical ordered set of outcomes specific to language learning.

In this study the teachers based their evaluative judgements on their internal reflective knowledge, as well as on the 1991 Victorian English Profiles (Ministry of Education and Training [School Programs Division], Victoria, 1991); the 1994 Western Australia First Steps Continua (Education Department of Western Australia, 1994a, 1994b, 1994c, 1994d), and the explicitly stated expectations from the *Curriculum and Standards Framework: English* (Board of Studies, Victoria, 1995). The teachers consistently referred to formative knowledge of student's literacy development and of using portfolios to build a profile of each student's achievements.

One of the teachers was more familiar than the other two with the CSF English levels and referred to them in her assessment practices but not her reporting procedures. All three teachers commented on the educational jargon in the CSF documentation. They all discussed the inappropriateness of using the CSF language in the report forms sent home to their students' parents. All three teachers spoke openly about the importance of assessing the individual student. The need to comparatively assess students' literacy achievements against other students, or to externally established student norms, was of no apparent interest to the teachers in this study. Consequently, they did not use Norm Referenced Tests (NRT) to establish reference standards of literacy achievement. The teachers' stated opposition to using NRTs complements their theoretical beliefs in the psycholinguistic principles of language learning.

The use of the CSF levels of achievement is not reflected in the case-study schools' curriculum policy documents. However, this is not an unexpected result as the CSF was only released in draft form in 1994. The published version of the CSF was sent to Victorian schools in 1995, the year the data collection for this study commenced. Accordingly, one would not expect a document to be incorporated into the curriculum publications of Victorian schools in the year that the DoE officially requested school personnel to become familiar with the document. During the 1995 interviews the teachers commented on whether or not they would change their student report forms. There was some reluctance to commit themselves to this procedure. Victoria commented that it would be in direct opposition to the school's policy of not supporting comparative assessment practices. Georgina commented that if the DoE required this practice then teachers would be forced to comply. This in fact was what did happen. In 1996 the

DSE sent out Directive 96/021 stating quite clearly that schools were required to report to parents using the CSF levels.

In 1997 I returned to all three case-study schools and collected a new set of report forms. All three schools had added the appropriate CSF levels to the front page of each report form. The influence on teachers' literacy judgements of external requirements is clearly apparent from this example. The powerful influence of compulsion should not be underestimated. However, is there a difference between a directive that is undertaken through compliance and a directive that results in changes in curriculum planning and delivery? Ascertaining the effectiveness of compulsion, in terms of literacy assessment and reporting practices, is another study in itself. The teachers have complied with the DoE directive. Their 1995 concerns regarding the inappropriateness of the language of the CSF for reporting purposes may have been a reaction because of their unfamiliarity with the documents. Their concerns may have dissipated as a result of the CSF familiarization processes, and of the use of the CSF achievement levels with students and parents. However, once again the powerful influence of the macropolitical sphere on the daily classroom practices of teachers is evidenced in this research. The political notion of summative assessment and benchmark testing, in relation to accountability practices, is inconsistent with the teachers' beliefs in formative assessment and reporting.

Political context

The political context in which the teachers work should not be underestimated as a powerful influence upon their literacy judgements. The reigning political climate influences not only what they assess as literacy, but also when and how literacy is assessed and reported. Throughout the entire data-collection process issues related to the influence of the political context over teachers' literacy judgements were evident and documented. The teachers spoke of the quality of the Western Australian programme known as *First Steps* (Education Department of Western Australia, 1994a, 1994b, 1994c, 1994d). However, they acknowledged the DoE (Department of Education, Victoria) directive to use the *Curriculum and Standards Framework (CSF): English* (Board of Studies, Victoria, 1995). The teachers spoke of their use of multiple sources of outcomes-based reference criteria regarding their literacy expectations (Ministry of Education [School Program Division], Victoria, 1990; Ministry of Education [School Program Division], Victoria, 1991; Ministry of Education, Victoria, 1988). However, they were very conscious of the DSE (Department of School Education) directive to use the LAP (Learning Assessment Project) and report to parents using the CSF levels. The overriding issue of funding to schools was noted on several occasions as the reason why certain literacy-assessment strategies could not be used.

Summary statement

A number of major conclusions can be drawn from this research. First, internalized reflective knowledge is a powerful influence on teachers' judgements of students' literacy development. This concept is a comprehensive term encompassing various other terms used in the literature on teacher judgement: tacit knowledge, intuition, common sense, personal experience, and personal theory. The use of the term *internalized reflective knowledge* conceptualizes the nature of the act and adds meaning to the complex cognitive processes involved.

Secondly, the research confirms that a diverse range of assessment strategies is used to ascertain literacy development in the three case-study schools. The study also demonstrates that at the classroom level there is an ideological integrity in the relationship between literacy-assessment techniques chosen and the theoretical model of literacy learning that underpins the teachers' literacy curriculum planning.

Thirdly, the research describes connections in relation to the influence of experts, significant others, and influential peers on teachers' decision-making processes. The study raises a number of issues about choice and compulsion related to literacy assessment and reporting practices.

Fourthly, the study highlights the complex nature of accountability issues in the educational community. The three case-study teachers articulated a strong belief that accountability can be demonstrated through formative and school-based contextualised literacy assessment. However, the findings also illustrate that standards and literacy expectations based on summative practices are externally imposed upon teachers and schools, and within this broad political climate conformity is a reality.

Fifthly, the all-encompassing political context is identified as a powerful influential feature not only imposing constraints upon teachers' judgements of students' literacy development, but also contributing to change at the system and school level.

Implications for educational practice

Each of these conclusions has important implications for educational practice at the school, tertiary preservice, and post-initial training levels. A number of recommendations are made; each is relevant not only to teachers at the classroom and school levels, but also to administrators at the policy level in the education system, as well as those involved in teacher education and professional development.

Moderation practices and teachers articulating their beliefs to enhance professional expertise

Effective teacher judgement of literacy assessment will be enhanced by practices that facilitate moderation between teachers. The research data in this thesis point to the beneficial nature of the practice of asking teachers to articulate their beliefs, their classroom routines, and the relationship of these activities to theoretical foundations. If teachers are encouraged to articulate what is effectively their internalized reflective knowledge, not only will they develop their professional competence to relate practice and theory, but they will also build up their knowledge base by sharing judgements. Professional development activities that require teachers to explain and share their decision-making judgements in collaborative networks need to be developed.

Interschool exchange of literacy assessment and reporting practices

Related to the issue of moderation is the need to facilitate communication channels between primary schools and secondary schools regarding literacy assessment practices. The data collected on the influence on teachers' judgements of transition requirements from secondary schools highlight the need for system collaboration. The teachers in this study were systematically collecting assessment data requested by the secondary school the Year 6 students were to attend the following year, in some cases bypassing the data already collected on the students' literacy achievements. The teachers were administering scholarship tests that did not reflect their philosophical principles about teaching and learning. However, the need to support their students, who were inexperienced in a testing environment, outweighed the teachers' own assessment beliefs. There is an obvious need for primary and secondary schools to communicate and collaborate on assessment and reporting information needs in the transition Years 6 and 7.

Changes in policy to school and education system professional development and tertiary institution preservice and post–initial training

The relationship between teachers' selection of assessment strategies and their philosophical beliefs about English language learning has important

Understanding the influences on teachers' judgements in the process of assessing and reporting students' literacy in the classroom

27

implications for policy development not only at the school and system levels, but also for tertiary training institutions with regard to professional development practices.

Examination of the teachers' qualifications in this study revealed that they had all been trained in the early literacy inservice course (ELIC) in the late 1980s. Ten years later these teachers still strongly believe in the theoretical principles taught through the ELIC programme. The ELIC programme was considered to be one of the most successfully implemented professional development packages in psycholinguistic beliefs in English language learning, and the very effective implementation strategies have been influential in the teaching and learning strategies incorporated in the classroom practices of many teachers, not only in Victoria.

The combination of the power of internal reflective knowledge with the effect of teachers articulating their professional knowledge could enhance their understanding of literacy-assessment practices. This raises a number of issues regarding professional development practices. At the school level, professional development planning that capitalizes on moderation activities may be instrumental in developing teachers' professional competence. Moderation strategies that incorporate teachers articulating their professional understanding of literacy assessment and reporting could enhance the implementation of coherent, school-based literacy development. Addressing issues such as the following would be invaluable discussion for school policy development:

- the literacy-judgement criteria teachers use,
- the literacy-assessment techniques teachers use,
- the literacy expectations teachers hold for a diverse range of students,
- the public benchmark literacy standards used in large-scale testing programmes in Australia,
- the philosophical beliefs about English language acquisition and learning, and
- the teaching and learning principles and their relationship to the assessment-reporting practices of individual schools.

At the system policy level, investigating professional programmes that incorporate teacher articulation as a key element in the package may well produce the most effective inservice. Clear recommendations regarding the essential nature of professional development for the teaching profession are made in *Literacy for All: The Challenge for Australian Schools*, the 1998 Commonwealth literacy policies for Australian schools monograph. One finds comments such as the following: "...the need for increased opportunity for teachers to have access to meaningful professional development" (p. 28); and "...provision of adequate professional development for teachers is also essential when implementing new strategies..." (p. 28).

The research in this study opens up the possibility of another dimension to teachers' professional development. Teachers articulating their practices and understandings may enhance the effectiveness of professional development programmes. New ways of involving teachers in their own professional development need to be researched. The transmission model of passing on expert advice may not be maximizing either the incorporation of that advice, or the internal reflective knowledge of teachers.

The current research also raises questions in relation to tertiary institutions specializing in the preservice and post-initial training of teachers. The identification of internalized reflective knowledge as a powerful influence on teachers' judgements of students' literacy development needs to be nurtured in novice teachers and extended in experienced practitioners. Tertiary teaching practices that require teachers in training to understand and develop their own internalized reflective knowledge may add to the number of teachers in the field of the caliber of Alexandra, Georgina, and Victoria. Tertiary teaching practices that involve student teachers articulating their beliefs in a public arena, defending their judgement and decision-making practices in debate situations, and demonstrating the evidence on which their literacy decisions are based would be valuable additions to this teaching and learning environment.

Notes

1. K.10.3. refers to KWALITAN notation Document 10, Segment 3, in the interview data.
2. ITQ–PB–Q1 refers to Initial Teacher Questionnaire, part B, Question 1.

REFERENCES

Anthony, R.J., Johnson, T.D., Mickelson, N.I., & Preece, A. (1991). *Evaluating literacy: A perspective for change.* Port Melbourne, Victoria, Australia: Rigby Heinemann.

Berliner, D.C. (1986, August/September). In pursuit of the expert pedagogue. *Educational Researcher, 15*(7), 5–13.

Board of Studies Victoria. (1995). *Curriculum and standards framework: English.* Carlton, Victoria, Australia: Author.

Bullock, A., Sir (Chairman). (1975). *A Language for life: Report of the Committee of Inquiry appointed by the Secretary of State for Education and Science.* London: Her Majesty's Stationery Office.

Cambourne, B.L., & Turbill, J. (Eds.), (1994). *Responsive evaluation: Making valid judgements about student literacy.* Armadale, Victoria, Australia: Eleanor Curtain.

Christie, F. (1991, August). *Teaching English literacy: A project of national significance on the pre-service preparation of teachers for teaching English literacy.* Canberra, Australian Capital Territory: Department of Employment Education and Training.

Denzin, N.K., & Lincoln, Y.S. (Eds.). (1994). *Handbook of qualitative research.* Thousand Oaks, CA: Sage.

Department of Employment, Education and Training. (1991). *Australia's language: The Australian language and literacy policy.* Canberra, Australian Capital Territory: Author.

Department of Employment, Education, Training and Youth Affairs. (1998). *Literacy for all: The challenge for Australian schools* (Commonwealth literacy policies for Australian schools). Canberra, Australian Capital Territory: Author.

Dilena, M., & van Kraayenoord, C.E. (1995, May). Whole school approaches to assessing and reporting literacy. *The Australian Journal of Language and Literacy, 18*(2), 136–143.

Dilena, M., & van Kraayenoord, C.E. (1996a). *Whole school approaches to assessing and reporting literacy: Children's literacy projects 1993–1994* (Final report. Executive summary). Canberra, Australian Capital Territory: Commonwealth Department of Employment, Education, Training and Youth Affairs, Targeted Programs Branch.

Dilena, M., & van Kraayenord, C.E. (1996b). *Whole school approaches to assessing and reporting literacy: Children's literacy projects 1993–1994* (Final report. Vol. 1: Case studies). Canberra, Australian Capital Territory: Department of Employment, Education, Training and Youth Affairs.

Education Department of Western Australia. (1994a). *First steps: Oral developmental continuum.* Melbourne, Victoria, Australia: Longman Cheshire.

Education Department of Western Australia. (1994b). *First steps: Reading developmental continuum.* Melbourne, Victoria, Australia: Longman Cheshire.

Education Department of Western Australia. (1994c). *First steps: Spelling developmental continuum.* Melbourne, Victoria, Australia: Longman Cheshire.

Education Department of Western Australia. (1994d). *First steps: Writing developmental continuum.* Melbourne, Victoria, Australia: Longman Cheshire.

Elbaz, F. (1981, Spring). The teachers' "practical knowledge": Report of a case study. *Curriculum Inquiry, 11*(1), 43–71.

Forster, M., & Masters, G. (1996). *Assessment resources kit: Performances.* Camberwell, Victoria, Australia: Australian Council for Educational Research.

Gee, J.P. (1991). What is literacy? In C. Mitchell & K. Weiler (Eds.), *Rewriting literacy: Culture and the discourse of the other* (pp. 3–11). New York: Bergin & Garvey.

Green, B., Hodgens, J., & Luke, A. (1994a). *Debating literacy in Australia: A documentary history, 1945–1994* (Vol. 1). Carlton, Victoria, Australia: Australian Literacy Federation.

Green, B., Hodgens, J., & Luke, A. (1994b). *Debating literacy in Australia: A documentary history, 1945–1994* (Vol. 2). Carlton, Victoria, Australia: Australian Literacy Federation.

Green, B., Hodgens, J., & Luke, A. (1997, February). Debating literacy in Australia: History lessons and popular f(r)ictions. *The Australian Journal of Language and Literacy, 29*(1), 6–24.

Guba, E.G., & Lincoln, Y.S. (1994). Competing paradigms in qualitative research. In N.K. Denzin & Y.S. Lincoln (Eds.), *Handbook of qualitative research* (Ch. 6, pp. 105–117). Thousand Oaks, CA: Sage.

Hargreaves, D.H. (1977). A phenomenological approach to classroom decision-making. Cambridge *Journal of Education, 7*(1), Lent Term, 12–20.

Hill, P.W., & Crevola, C.A.M. (1997, November). *The literacy challenge in Australian primary schools* (Seminar Series No. 69). Melbourne, Victoria, Australia: Incorporated Association of Registered Teachers of Victoria (IARTV).

ISYS. (1988a). *ISYS for Windows: Administration & utilities manual*. Version 4.0. [Computer software]. Greenwood Village, CO: Odyssey Development.

ISYS. (1988b). *ISYS for Windows: Query user's manual*. Version 4.0. [Computer software]. Greenwood Village, CO: Odyssey Development.

Kennedy, K.J., & Hodgens, J. (1989). Focusing on teacher quality in the quest for higher standards: The early literacy inservice course. *Journal Curriculum Studies, 21*(5), 409–425.

Lankshear, C., Gee, J.P., Knobel, M., & Searle, C. (1997). *Changing literacies*. Buckingham, England: Open University Press.

Luke, A., & Gilbert, P. (Eds.). (1993). *Literacy in context: Australian perspectives and issues*. St. Leonards, New South Wales, Australia: Allen & Unwin.

Masters, G., & Forster, M. (1996). *Assessment resource kit: Developmental assessment*. Camberwell, Victoria, Australia: Australian Council for Educational Research.

Ministry of Education (School Programs Division), Victoria. (1990). *Literacy profiles handbook: Assessing and reporting literacy development*. Melbourne, Victoria, Australia: Author.

Ministry of Education and Training (School Programs Division), Victoria. (1991). *English profiles handbook: Assessing and reporting students' progress in English*. Melbourne, Victoria, Australia: Author.

Ministry of Education, Victoria. (1988). *The English language framework P–10*. Melbourne, Victoria, Australia: Author.

Moni, K.B., Tonkin, L., & van Kraayenoord, C.E. (1996). *Whole school approaches to assessing and reporting literacy. Children's literacy projects 1993–1994* (Final report. Vol. 2: Practices in project schools). Canberra, Australian Capital Territory: Department of Employment, Education, Training and Youth Affairs.

New London Group, The. (1996, Spring). A pedagogy of multiliteracies: Designing social futures. *Harvard Educational Review, 66*(1), 60–91.

Peters, V., & Wester, F. (1990, June). *Qualitative analysis in practice* (Including user's guide Kwalitan Version 2). Nijmegen, The Netherlands: University of Nijmegen, Social Sciences Faculty, Department of Research Methodology.

Peters, V., & Wester, F. (1993, May). *Qualitative analysis in practice. Supplement* (A short help to learn Version 3.1). [Computer Software]. Nijmegen, The Netherlands: University of Nijmegen, Social Science Faculty, Department of Research Methodology.

Shulman, L.S. (1987, February). Knowledge and teaching: Foundations of the new reform. *Harvard Educational Review, 57*(1), 1–22.

Stiggins, R.J., & Conklin, N.F. (1992). *In teachers' hands: Investigating the practices of classroom assessment*. Albany, NY: State University of New York Press.

Understanding the influences on teachers' judgements in the process of assessing and reporting students' literacy in the classroom

31

Assessing information literacy: A reception class learns the skills and how to assess their learning

Kate Mount

At the same time that I plan to teach the skills of information literacy, I set up my record for observing these skills.

My observation checklist is based on the eight separate information literacy skills that I teach. These skills are:

1. Articulate and record known facts.
2. Form own questions.
3. Locate information.
4. Write clear answers and illustrate.
5. Organise a report booklet with a contents page and other features.
6. Present information effectively.
7. Evaluate own presentation.
8. Monitor own progress.

Every year I spend each term on a unit of information literacy with my reception class. Some of the topics I have focused on have been Space, The Farm, The Body, Rainforests, and Fairytales. I have found that a unit on seeking, gathering, and presenting information allows me to teach the process in a fun and exciting manner, using an integrated approach to learning. The children, who have only just entered school, quickly become familiar with the process, as it is set out clearly and is such a supportive way to learn. The themes provide a high interest level and the unit of work is shared with the homes, the parents becoming involved in a variety of ways.

As a class we discuss the eight stages of the information process, and I list them on a chart to display for easy reference. I also set up the students with folders and their own list of the stages, so that they can monitor their own progress.

From *Practically Primary*, 2(1), March 1997. Reprinted with permission of the Australian Literacy Educators' Association.

At each stage of the process I make explicit the elements for effective achievement of that stage. For example, when they are preparing the research presentation, we discuss what a good presentation would be like. The following self-assessment sheet was prepared after one class agreed that for an effective presentation they needed to have a clear voice, eye contact with the audience or the speakers, focus on the information that they found, and to listen well.

I also need to plan opportunities to observe each student, such as during small group discussions on what the students know about a topic. I move around with my observation sheet on a clipboard and note the students' achievements. I also meet regularly with individual students to find out where they are up to in their process and assist those who need it.

Term 1 Research Presentation

3 very good	2 okay	1 not good
1. Using a loud clear voice	[loud]	3 2 ①①①
2. Using eye contact	[eyes]	3 2 ①
3. Sharing my information	Bones	3 2 ①
4. Being a good listener	[ear]	3 ② 1

Parent comment:

I was very impressed with Sally's model of a bone and the information she had found out. LP

Teacher Comment

Sally, we were all very interested in your facts about bones and how they grow. A clear presentation. Well done
K Mount

Criteria to be observed during information process	Is able to articulate and record facts they already know on topic.	Is able to formulate own questions appropriate to topic.	Is able to locate information using a variety of resources.	Is able to write clear answer to question and illustrate.	Is able to organise questions into a booklet using a contents page and one other extra.	Is able to present information in an interesting informative manner, e.g., diorama/talk.	Is able to evaluate own performance throughout the stages.	Is able to monitor own progress during process.
Alexander I-W	2		1→2	1				
Alexandra M	3 very artic.		1	1				
Andrew A	3 uses adv. vocab	✓	3	3				
Andrew H	3	✓	3	3				
Callum W	1 needs enc.		1	1				
Catherine A	1→2	✓	2	3				
Grace H	2		2	1→2				
Harry B-H	3 very comp.	✓	3	3				
Imogen N	3 articulate	✓	2	2+				
James M	1 needs encour.		1	1				
James V	2		2	1+				
James W	2 needs encour.		2	2				
Laura S	3 exc.	✓	3	3				
Mark V	3 mature vocab	✓	2→3	2→3				
Matthew F	3 artic.	✓	3	3				
Melanie T	3 very adv.	✓	3	3				
Nicholas B	3 confident	✓	2	2				
Philippa M	3 artic.	✓	2	2				
Rachael A-W	3 very artic.	✓	1→2	1→2				
Sarah S	2 needs encour.		1	1				
Sophie O	3 very artic.	✓	3	3				
Thomas E	3 very artic	✓	3	3				
Thomas N	2		2	2				
William B	2 better eye contact		2	2				
William M	3 adv. vocab	✓	3	3				

3–very well   2–okay   1–needs further help   ✔–have observed

At all stages of the process I plan for students to assess their own achievements, using criteria that we have worked out together.

At the making and presentation stage I take care to support the students with their constructions, whilst making sure that the final work is the students' own understanding of the information gathered.

There are three considerations that I have found important in making the learning successful. They are:

1. The checklist must be manageable, so I adjust it to meet the particular students' needs.

2. I need to be explicit to myself and to the students about exactly what it is I am observing.

3. I must make time to gain the students' own perceptions of their achievements.

Whenever I use this process I am constantly amazed how focused the young learners are on the task at hand. They are accurately able to assist in the evaluation process. From this we are able to set achievable goals for the next term so that the children and their parents can see the growth points, using the Information Literacy framework. The children have a strong desire to achieve on an individual level and feel personally rewarded for their efforts.

Assessing information literacy:
A reception class learns
the skills and how
to assess their learning
35

Students assess their own reporting and presentation skills

Ros Fryar

I have been using student assessment with upper primary students for many years, because I believe that students are empowered as learners when they are involved in setting their own criteria and use the criteria to make judgements about their own work. The whole process means that the students and teachers come to use the same language and agree on what they are aiming for in the learning activity. The teacher becomes more of a facilitator, with the students taking more responsibility for the entire learning process: the planning, the doing, and the assessing.

Planning

As part of the research process I generally plan to develop and assess writing as well as speaking outcomes related to students' presentation of their research findings. The particular outcomes that I aim for depend on the skills that the students already have in oral presentation and in written reports. But at years 6 and 7 my focus is usually on students' selection and organisation of information, the range of resources they have used, and their success in presenting to an audience. Students are often given the opportunity to prepare and present their oral reports as a group. It is important, however, to vary group with individual work so that all students have a chance to work in their preferred way.

Once I have determined and recorded the outcomes, I plan the teaching activities to reach these outcomes. I know that I must plan extra time to allow for negotiating the criteria, for the students to assess their work, or have a teacher–student or peer conference before the final report is made.

Identifying the criteria

The process of establishing the criteria for assessment is much the same whether it is in report writing, oral presentations, or any other activity.

From *Practically Primary*, 21(1), March 1997. Reprinted with permission of the Australian Literacy Educators' Association.

First the teacher explains the activity that is to be assessed, the purpose of the students assessing their own work, and the need to decide together on the aspects that are to be considered for assessment. The students soon realise that the criteria they are negotiating are the aspects they need to aim for as they plan and complete their work.

The whole class then brainstorm the criteria that should be considered. Emphasis is placed on the students being specific. I ask them what they mean by "good" when they say "having good facial expressions" and what sorts of notes would be useful when they say "uses notes."

All suggestions in the brainstorming should be accepted and recorded, without comment or discussion. The class then selects the criteria that will be used. Consideration is given to the learning outcomes that have been planned, what is manageable for the students, the year level, and past experience. The class then discusses how the criteria will be measured: by a rating scale of, for example, 1 to 5; with comments only; or present or not present.

Once the method of assessment is agreed, the next step is to decide who will prepare the assessment proforma and when it will be needed. Generally two or three students do this cooperatively, based on an assessment form that the class has used before. The following two proforma were to assess a group's oral report and a written report.

ORAL REPORT		Date ...August..9t.
GROUP MEMBERS...Lynda B Cut M Jodie S Michelle W...		MY ROLE ...Recorder...
Research Report	**Comments**	**Group assessment**
Text: Report		these are things we did well
Prepare report showing • organisation, • appropriate content • use of headings •	good organisation changed to own words	– all had a part – worked well in group
Contextual understanding • clear introduction • language audience expected and understood • terminology explained • looked at audience	We all faced audience and were understood. Writing up research title a good idea	– good presentation
Linguistic structure & features • pace • volume • expression •	Voices clear, fluent and at right pace Lynda needed more expression	Things we need to improve on – standing and showing interest when others speak. Conclusion clearer.
Strategies • use of visual aids • reference to notes only • used feedback given before • organisation of group • good use of group	We did change our report from feedback. Jodie introduced and finished.	

Students assess their own reporting and presentation skills

37

Practice in using the criteria

Prior to the presentations or at the last draft stage of a written report the criteria are revisited. With oral presentations, rehearsal time is given along with the opportunity for a teacher–student conference or peer feedback, using the agreed criteria. With written reports, writing conferences or peer feedback are just as applicable. If peer feedback is used it is advisable to have students write their specific feedback for each other, and for the teacher to ask students what they need to work on to improve on the agreed criteria.

Presentations and assessments

Students complete their written assessments as soon as possible after their oral presentations or just before passing up their written work.

Opportunities are given for students to share their own assessments with each other and the teacher. The teacher then adds comments to the completed self-assessments and, where appropriate, asks the students for evidence of meeting the criteria. The completed proforma is included in the students' portfolios or take-home books. These are sent home, and parents are invited to add their comments in the space provided.

Final self-assessment and goal setting

Once all aspects of the research process have been completed, the skills learnt and needing development are revisited with another self-assessment proforma (see the example). The proforma can be developed with the whole class and revisited each time a research project is undertaken over a year, with special attention given to the goal set.

My Research Checklist

Name: . . . . Date: . . . .

Research topic: . . . .

The topic was presented as a:

☐ poster   ☐ written report
☐ interview   ☐ video-tape
☐ illustration   ☐ brochure
☐ article   ☐ book

After completing my research I can:	not well	average	quite well
• list what I already know			
• frame questions that I want to follow			
• contribute when brainstorming the topic			
• use the library to find suitable resources			
• find suitable books and pages to answer my questions			
• identify other resources (people, newspapers, computer)			
• select the best resources to use			
• take notes that address my questions			
• listen carefully to answers to questions			
• summarise information			
• organise the information collected			
• organise my time			
• work alone on some areas			
• work with others cooperatively			
• show responsibility			
• prepare the presentation			
• present the information			

Goal setting

For my next research topic I aim to . . . .

. . . .

Students assess their own reporting and presentation skills

Children's self evaluations

Robyn Perkins

Children across eight grades from three schools—St Mary's Ascot Vale, Bank St Ascot Vale, and Moonee Ponds West—were given the following question: How do you show your teacher when you've learned something? They reflected on what's important to them, how they know when they're learning. Their responses are in themselves an authentic assessment.

Jordan: "I reckon that how to show the teacher how you are going with your work is to show them what you have done and tell them and try to do your best work. And I think that I have done all of that stuff."

Rani: "I talk to the teacher about my work."

Jessica: "I think it's important that people say what they think in their self evaluation."

Mikaela: "Self evaluations show what you like and sometimes things you like you're good at. When you get a piece of writing from this year and from last year you can tell you've improved."

Pat: "I don't show it at all."

Freya: "When I learn something I look back in the past and remember the things I have learnt."

Laura: "I know I am learning because I have a go. I feel confident and get more challenged which makes me learn. I practise a lot and learn what I practiced. I learn from my mistakes."

Elizabeth: "People say 'well done'. I get excited. When I learn something I want to keep doing the same thing."

Isaac: "I can draw to show what I learnt."

From "Chatterbox," *Practically Primary*, 4(1), February 1999. Reprinted with permission of the Australian Literacy Educators' Association.

Sean draws to describe his progress:

"last year"

this is lots yolaat

this is this year Utat.

year

Kelly: "Sometimes people will tell you that you have improved. Sometimes I might have a go at something. I might be reading a book and I might not have read it before because I thought it was too hard. Then I know I have learnt something."

Jesse: "If I am doing better at something I tend to do a lot more of it."

Katherine: "You look really astonished. You raise your eyebrows. Sometimes you tell someone (a friend)."

Debbie: "In maths it depends on what subject it is. In plus I'm good but sometimes I get confused. A way to show is to get some numbers and for me to tell or show how I worked it out. That's the same with all the other maths. For friends, it would be how many friends I have, if I'm friendly with a lot of people."

Cameron: "When I am reading I read longer books and that means that I am learning to read more words. When I am writing I spell the words how I think they are spelt, and then I have a conference and look at the words that are wrong and sometimes I look in the dictionary and proof read."

when i Get home i think of one or two Things that i Learnt that Day.

when i complete work i Look at my work and see The difference in it.

my Body feels. Good.

By James

Tom: • "When it looks good."
        • "When it looks better."
        • "When I find it interesting."
        • "When I want to keep going."
        • "When I work hard."
        • "When I make mistakes."
        • "When I ask for help."

Chris: "I say in my mind, have I learnt something. I look on this note in my mind and see if I have learnt something."

Fabien: "I was doing a really hard sum and I just worked it out in my head."

Alinta: "Your literature book shows how you're going at reading. Conferences help kids and teachers. It helps teachers by looking with their own eyes. [Assessment] files help because they show drafts from the start to the finish of the year."

Hannah: "You can show your parents at parent/child/teacher interview. You can show things like self evaluation, personal writing project book and file."

Matthew: "When I learnt something I go up to the teachers at the end of the session and tell them."

Sophie: "I take my book out to the teacher and explain what I did."

Emily: "Well you can tell with handwriting because the drafts are better and the published copy is neater and in maths you can tell if kids have improved because they challenge themselves with harder problems. It's pretty dumb learning the same thing over and over again."

Amanda: "I will do my best work and my best spelling. If my teacher says it is not very good I will cry and I will be very sad for all of the day."

Jessie: "You draw and label things to show the parts. You write to show you learn. You have a go, then you get it conferenced to see if you've learnt something. In your first year your writing is OK. In your second year, it's better."

Erin: "I can read better this year because when I was little I would be reading things like cat, dog, happy. But now I am reading lots of harder things and I can teach my little sister and I am proud of it."

Daniel: "I show by looking back on my work say 'literature' and talking about how interesting the book was. *101 Wacky Facts About Bugs* and *Spiders and Snakes and Reptiles* were more interesting than *Walk twenty, run twenty*. I also look at how I published early in the year and how I publish late in the year. I do similar things with maths, projects and writing."

Robbie: "When someone asks you a question and you answer it straight away."

Evelyn: "Last year I could only read four words: the, do, it, is. This year I can read Pony pals books by myself—one of the words was 'dismantled.'
"Writing: I'm getting better at leaving spaces, you can see them in my writing this year."

Tegan: "You know something you didn't know before."

Toward self-assessment of literacy learning

Christina E. van Kraayenoord

Children can be motivated and engaged in literacy learning to a greater degree when they play more active roles in the assessment of their accomplishments. Although teachers traditionally have been the major source of information about literacy development, pupils should also be seen as significant contributors to the process of assessment. One way in which this can be done is for children to be engaged in self-assessment of their literacy development.

Self-assessment involves self-reflection and self-evaluation, which may both be viewed as metacognitive skills (Paris & Winograd, 1990). When pupils have authentic purposes for engaging in literacy activities in the classroom, self-assessment requires that they think about their knowledge, skills, and attitudes in a variety of literacy contexts. Self-assessment also means that the students evaluate their knowledge and skills in relation to previous personal performance or feelings, or to standards and criteria of achievement.

The role of the pupil in assessment in classrooms

Self-assessment provides an opportunity for pupils to think about their learning and to create knowledge about themselves as learners. The knowledge that is created is "knowledge that informs their understandings and those of their teacher about what they have achieved" (Gomez, Graue, & Bloch, 1991, p. 626). Both the processes of literacy learning and the products of literacy learning can be thought about and evaluated. The information from self-assessment can be used to maintain and confirm feelings, to develop new goals for learning, and to act as an impetus to seek help with further learning.

Self-assessment offers several advantages to pupils. Firstly, it allows them to assess what they have learned, that is, to come to understand what they know. Secondly, it informs them about how they are doing, providing them with a "progress report" of their learning. Thirdly, self-assessment

From *The Australian Journal of Language and Literacy*, 17(1), February 1994. Reprinted with permission of the Australian Literacy Educators' Association.

allows pupils to discover how they learn best by finding out which procedures worked and which did not, and under what conditions. In order to help children acquire these benefits of self-assessment, teachers need to know what children should be asked to self-assess.

What should be assessed?

Deciding what should be assessed is an important aspect of literacy instruction. Teachers and pupils should be assessing the "dimensions of literacy learning" that are valued (van Kraayenoord & Paris, 1992). The dimensions are features of literacy learning that represent knowledge, skills, and attitudes considered to be important by the teachers, school administration, and parents. They reflect views about learning and/or literacy theory and the curriculum, and what occurs in classrooms and in instruction. The children know what the dimensions are because they are explicit (Paris, Calfee, Filby, Hiebert, Pearson, Valencia, & Wolf, 1992; Valencia, Au, Scheu, & Kawakami, 1990; van Kraayenoord & Paris, 1992).

Teachers often ask pupils to assess their spelling or handwriting, but self-assessment of literacy should not be limited to the mechanics of production or accuracy of performance alone. A critical function of self-assessment is to make pupils more engaged in their own reading and writing by viewing their performance as personal—something they control and a reflection of their own thoughts and feelings. Thus, in this article the focus is on two dimensions of literacy, ownership and responsibility, although there are many other dimensions that could be used as the basis for pupils to evaluate their literacy. Ownership and responsibility have been selected because they are aspects of literacy learning that should be valued, because they should be evident in many situations where children are engaged in literacy instruction, and because they foster the participation of children in self-regulated learning.

Ownership

One critical dimension of literacy instruction is that of ownership. In becoming competent readers and writers, children should be actively engaged in learning about literacy as well as through literacy. They can display a sense of ownership by making choices about what they read and write, by deciding what and how to contribute to classroom activities, and by sharing their achievements, knowledge, and feelings. Ownership is fostered when pupils are part of the process of assessment. By being actively involved in assessing their learning, students are encouraged to think about their own work and to respond to it. Opportunities to reflect about the products and processes of learning create a sense of personal ownership.

Ownership is engendered through assessment when children are able to reflect on what they can do rather than what they can not; a focus on success and not failure. Ownership is also developed when children see that the classroom assessment activities are meaningful and relevant to them. When children are asked directly to provide information themselves they can see that assessment is a "reasonable process" (Tierney, Carter, & Desai, 1991). Because they are actually involved in the process of assessment themselves, children are more likely to see the connection between the assessment activities and their own learning.

The feelings of ownership will lead to a greater commitment to learning and the goals of instruction. The children will feel that they are real participants in the literacy activities and that the work that they produce shows what they are capable of doing. Ownership is demonstrated when pupils reveal attitudes that show that they believe that the reading and writing activities they are doing are important. Their commitment to literacy learning and assessment will also lead to a sense of pride. Children who value the process, the products, and themselves in assessment will develop a sense of pride (Linek, 1991). They will feel good about themselves and confident about their increased control over what they are learning. The sense of pride will be a powerful force in helping children face new literacy learning tasks with confidence and effort.

Responsibility

A second dimension of literacy learning is that of responsibility. Responsibility can be viewed as ownership in action. It involves pupils' attributions and their belief that they have control of and have authority over their own learning. It is concerned with setting goals, making choices, and decision making.

Responsibility can be fostered when children can attribute the assessment of the learning process to themselves, rather than to the teachers as external agents (Lamme & Hysmith, 1991). If teachers solely do the assessing it suggests to the pupils that only these individuals have "the skill and expertise to evaluate students' work, and that this skill is not transferable" (Sadler, 1989). When teachers are the sole sources of assessment data, then it implies that teachers "know best", that they have the answers, and that they are the authority (Flanigan, 1986).

When teachers encourage attributions to pupils' appropriate and strategic efforts, then pupils will feel a sense of personal power over their accomplishments. Activities that allow children to make attributions to strategies will also foster responsibility. Planning and monitoring behaviours lead to feelings of involvement and control. When pupils are encouraged to set their own goals they will feel that their self-reflective evaluations are purposeful. They will see that their needs become their future goals, which in turn motivates them to achieve.

Responsibility can have a number of consequences. Allowing children to participate in decision making about literacy learning demonstrates to pupils that teachers value what students know and can do. Because self-assessment helps students discover where they have improved, as well as where further improvement is necessary, it encourages them to think about how they can learn more and how they can learn more effectively (Heath & Manigold, 1991). When self-assessment is coupled with decision making, the learner focuses on self-improvement. Therefore, responsibility about learning directs future learning and self-improvement.

The responsibility that pupils take for their own learning can also lead to discussions about what constitutes progress, of standards and criteria for good work. Such discussions mean that children can be involved in developing standards and in seeing how standards change and evolve. It is likely that when children are aware of and understand the descriptions of progress or criteria in reading and writing tasks they will be more committed and motivated to achieve them.

Classroom tasks to foster self-assessment

Knowledge of ownership and responsibility in reading, writing, speaking, and listening can be fostered by engaging children in a variety of self-assessment activities. In this section some activities will be described which show how teachers can foster self-assessment. These pupil activities include: (1) reviewing artefacts; (2) understanding progress through record keeping; (3) documenting interests, choices, and preferences; (4) conferences with teachers; (5) collaborative writing; and (6) sharing personal responses.

Reviewing artefacts

Many classroom teachers now employ portfolios of students' work. These are principled collections of evidence of the critical dimensions of literacy, the goals of the language arts curriculum, and children's literacy development (van Kraayenoord & Paris, 1992). Tierney, Carter, and Desai (1991) have argued that the major goal of portfolios is to promote self-assessment.

Students can be engaged in self-assessment as they select artefacts for their portfolios. In addition, conferences around portfolios are ideal settings for undertaking self-assessment of work that has been collected. An examination of a portfolio with a teacher provides an opportunity to obtain information about a particular aspect of a pupil's learning. Pupils can discuss their strengths and needs, as well as their attitudes to the topic which is the focus of the conference. While initially the teacher may select the focus, over time students should be encouraged to suggest the focus for the conference themselves. Students can also keep a record of decisions made during conferences. Having students choose the focus and recording the decisions means that what occurs during and after conferences is seen as their responsibility (Weeks & Leaker, 1991).

Understanding progress through record keeping

Another way in which children can engage in self-assessment is through keeping records of their reading, writing, and listening. Records of their work can be made via reading and writing logs, goal statements, report cards, and journals. These activities allow pupils to keep track of what they have read, written, heard, and seen, and their reactions and feelings across time. For example, in reading logs, pupils might record titles, authors, comments about the books, and ratings of books they have read. An illustration of a reading log can be found in Queensland Department of Education's *Years 1–10 English Language Arts: Assessment Guide* (1991). When records are systematically kept, and regularly used, then children can examine what they have written and read and begin to describe changes or lack of change based on information contained in the records.

Documenting interests, choices, and preferences

There are a number of measures that can help pupils document their interests, choices and preferences in literacy activities. Pupils can become more self-reflective by using measures that ask questions or ask for reactions to statements about learning, about choosing literacy activities in the classroom and at home, and about themselves as readers, writers, speakers, and listeners.

Rating scales, questionnaires, checklists, and inventories are measures that allow children to make self-assessments using a variety of response modes. For example, student's perceptions of themselves as readers and writers can be assessed using open-ended questionnaires focusing on their preferences, strengths, and weaknesses in reading and writing. An illustration of an open-ended questionnaire that taps these characteristics in writing can be found in South Australian Department of Education's *Literacy Assessment in Practice: R–7 Language Arts* (1991).

Conferences with teachers

Conferences with teachers are also useful tools to assist students in self-assessment. In a conference situation teachers can prompt children to self-assess by asking them about "Things I can do," "Things I am working on," and "Things I plan to learn" (based on Hansen, 1987). By using interview questions as guides, students can become aware of what they can do and in turn learn that they are responsible for that aspect of their learning.

Conferences can also be used to tap children's metacognitive awareness about reading. Myers and Paris (1978) have created an assessment tool that focusses on children's knowledge of person, task, and strategy variables on reading performance. This measure taps pupils' awareness of characteristics and strategies of effective readers. When used as a trigger to self-assessment, this measure of metacognition can assist teachers in obtaining insights into an important aspect of effective learning.

The Book Selection Task (Kemp, 1987) can also be used by teachers as a starting point for teacher–pupil conferences. The Book Selection Task allows children to provide reasons for liking or disliking a variety of books. Conferences around the Book Selection Task which focus on the reasons for choices would provide information about feelings and ownership.

Collaborative writing

Collaborative writing is a good place to introduce the concept of self-assessment. This is because writing involves the creation of an end product and a process of writing construction. Both the product and the process can be evaluated by pupils. While the products of writing can be self-assessed through the personal review of written artefacts, the processes of writing can be more difficult to self-assess.

One way in which self-assessment and the process of writing can be integrated is through the use of "think sheets" (Englert, 1990; Raphael & Englert, 1990). Think sheets are used to activate writing strategies for planning, organising, drafting, editing, and revising. The think sheets prompt the strategies for writing through the use of self-questions or self-instructions, scaffolding children's thinking by cueing them to particular strategies and activating self-assessment. Children can be encouraged to share their responses to their think sheets with a peer and to use the discussion of responses as feedback to improve aspects of their writing.

The use of think sheets promotes the important social features of collaboration. Children learn to share their thinking and their writing and learn to scaffold others as they try to shape their own work. They develop a respect for their peers, valuing their help and supporting each other.

Sharing personal responses

There are a number of instructional activities that provide an opportunity for students to react to what they have been listening to and reading, and to share those reactions with someone who responds to what they are thinking and feeling. Book reviews and peer reviews of published work provide opportunities for children to display their personal ideas and for others to respond to them.

"Authors' chair" is an instructional activity that provides an opportunity for children to share their reading or writing (Harste, Short, & Burke, 1988). Children can share a particular section of a story by reading it aloud to their classmates; often they begin or finish with a brief comment as to why the reading was selected. The author may also engage the listeners by asking them to participate by sharing their reactions to what was read.

Authors' chair principally emphasizes sharing, however in the process of sharing their own and others' texts, children often become aware of new or additional elements of what they have read or areas in which their writing can be improved or expanded. They can use the feedback from the other pupils to improve their writing or to elaborate their ideas.

Issues

In developing effective self-assessors, teachers may have some legitimate concerns. In this section, common question about self-assessment are raised and discussed.

How should the idea of self-assessment be introduced to children?

Teachers can make self-assessment part of their instruction by explaining to children what self-assessment is and its purposes. They can do this by helping students understand how their self-assessment information will be used and for what audiences, how it relates to other assessment information that is collected about them, and how the information leads to instructional decision making.

In addition to teacher explanation, teachers should explicitly instruct their pupils in the procedures of self-assessment, what Sadler (1989) has called "downloading of evaluative knowledge." Children need to know which aspects of literacy are important, be aware of the criteria and the performance levels in particular areas of literacy achievement, and know how to self-assess their own learning in light of the criteria.

Effective instruction about self-assessment can only occur when teachers have created classroom conditions in which children are encouraged to become self-assessors. This means that having a go at reflecting on and evaluating one's own work is seen as part of the learning process. The classroom tone is one in which students work knowing that they should engage in self-assessment and that they will be reinforced for doing so.

When should children begin self-assessment?

Teachers may ask whether or not young children can engage in self-assessment. There is some suggestion that because self-assessment requires higher level thinking, young children do not engage in it. Several authors, however, have argued that young children can evaluate themselves (e.g., Hansen, 1987; Sadler, 1989). While 5- and 6-year-olds can engage in assessment, as they get older they improve on the type of criteria they use to make self-appraisals, the complexity of their products, and their use of feedback to improve their performance.

Teachers can therefore introduce the notion of self-assessment in the early primary grades. When they embed self-assessment into instruction and demonstrate how it can be undertaken through modelling and thinking aloud, young children will quickly develop the idea of thinking about their learning.

Will all children participate equally in self-assessment?

Some authors have warned that not all children may participate equally in the assessment process. "Not all children have the same opportunities to generate products, and students vary in their ability to choose representations of their own learning" (Gomez, Graue, & Bloch, 1991). Thus teachers have to work hard to ensure that the children who may have difficulty with self-assessment are given additional opportunities to "generate products," to "choose representations," and to learn how to assess themselves. Children who cannot assess their performance will not know how to improve it, or know whether it deserves reward or criticism. These students will need extended support to learn how to make their self-monitoring effective. When children show that they are unable to make self-assessments of their own learning this should be seen as a signal to teachers of the need to include teaching about self-assessment in their instructional routines.

Is self-assessment always beneficial for children?

One of the concerns raised about the use of self-assessment activities is that for some children the results of self-evaluation may interfere with their learning and motivation. In particular, when children with poor literacy achievement or learning problems engage in self-assessment, they will establish for themselves that they are not doing well. Repeated self-assessment activities will confirm their poor achievement. This may lead to anxiety, fear, and low self-esteem. It is important for these students that teachers prevent them feeling badly about their self-assessments. This can be done in a number of ways. Firstly, it is important that children with difficulties learn how to assess using the goals and criteria of tasks. That means that the students need to be made aware of the goals and criteria and taught how to examine their achievement in light of them. Secondly, children need to be helped to focus on their growth, that is, on the changes in their own performance across time, so that they can remain optimistic about their personal progress. The emphasis should be on learning how to compare their own work of a similar type over several weeks, not on comparing their work with that of other students. Thirdly, teachers should focus on the children's efforts in learning and how the application of specific strategies will lead to greater learning effectiveness. By focusing on effort and strategic learning, teachers can communicate optimism for future achievement and growth.

Are all self-assessment tasks good measures?

Teachers need to be careful when selecting tasks that will be used by the pupils for self-assessment. Just because a task is labelled "self-assessment" or "self-evaluation" does not mean that it should be used. There are many tasks available that are untested, and for which we have little information as to their reliability or validity.

The same critical eye that teachers have when choosing instructional tasks needs to be used for self-assessment activities. First, only use tasks that are aligned with the "dimensions of literacy" that are valued. Secondly, only use tasks that are meaningful for the pupils, in that they are aware of the purposes. Thirdly, only use tasks where the items or questions are related to the goals of the task. Fourthly, consider what will be done with the information generated from the task. If nothing is done with the information, in an instructional sense, it may be better not to use it.

It is also important to try to find out about the origins of tasks. One writer has recently said "educators have to understand that it is not enough to say 'I designed this task and I say it is valid'.... We must be able to test any test against criteria just as we test each student's performance against criteria" (Wiggins, 1992, p. 36). Therefore, using the four criteria suggested above and examining the information about the measure's reliability and validity may be an important yardstick for selecting self-assessment activities.

Is self-assessment enough?

Self-assessment should not be the only form of assessment that is used in the classroom. While it was the intention of this article to draw attention to the need for teachers to include children directly as sources of assessment information, teachers and parents are also important sources. It would be dangerous to rely on one source of information to the exclusion of other sources. Assessment information should be collected from and shared collaboratively amongst teachers, children, and parents. When teachers, pupils, and parents contribute to assessment then all become partners in children's literacy learning.

Conclusion

Good classroom assessment incorporates self-assessment. Self-assessment is one aspect of the instruction and assessment practices which emerge from the valued dimensions of literacy learning. Self-assessment is an ideal vehicle to develop ownership and responsibility. When children are actively engaged in thinking about their performances, they will develop feelings of ownership that lead to beliefs about their own success, to motivated learning, and to commitment to the goals of learning. When pupils are encouraged to focus on their own learning and are invited to make decisions using the information that they have gained through their self-reflections, they will begin to assume responsibility. This in turn will lead to feelings of control over their literacy learning.

Note

1. 1 would like to acknowledge the help of Professor Scott Paris, University of Michigan, who discussed a number of the ideas in this article with me and for his suggestions related to drafting and revision.
2. A version of this article was given as a keynote address at the 38th Annual Convention of the International Reading Association, San Antonio, Texas, USA, 26–30 April, 1993.

REFERENCES

Englert, C.S. (1990). Unraveling the mysteries of writing through strategy instruction. In T.E. Scruggs & B.Y.L. Wong (Eds.), *Intervention research in learning disabilities* (pp. 186–223). New York: Springer Verlag.

Flanigan, M.C. (1986). Collaborative revision: Learning and self-assessment. In S. de Castell, A. Luke, & K. Egan (Eds.), *Literacy, society and schooling: A reader*. Cambridge: Cambridge University Press.

Gomez, M.L., Graue, M.E., & Bloch, M.N. (1991). Reassessing portfolio assessment: Rhetoric and reality. *Language Arts, 68*, 620–628.

Hansen, J. (1987). *When writers read.* Portsmouth, NH: Heinemann.

Harste, J.C., Short, K.G., & Burke, C. (1988). *Creating classrooms for authors: The reading–writing connection.* Portsmouth, NH. Heinemann.

Heath, S.B., & Manigold, L. (1991). *Children of promise: Literate activity in linguistically and culturally diverse classrooms.* Washington, DC: National Education Association.

Kemp, M. (1987). *Watching children read and write: Observational records for children with special needs.* Melbourne: Nelson.

Lamme, L.L., & Hysmith, C. (1991). One school's adventure into portfolio assessment. *Language Arts, 68*, 629–640.

Linek, W.M. (1991). Grading and evaluation techniques for whole language teachers. *Language Arts, 68*, 125–132.

Myers, M., & Paris, S.G. (1978). Children's metacognitive knowledge about reading. *Journal of Educational Psychology, 70*, 680–690.

Paris, S.G., Calfee, R.C., Filby, N., Hiebert, E., Pearson, D.O., Valencia, S.W., & Wolf, K.P. (1992). A framework for authentic literacy assessment. *The Reading Teacher, 46*, 88–98.

Paris, S.G., & Winograd, P. (1990). How metacognition can promote academic learning and instruction. In B.J. Jones & L. Idol (Eds.), *Dimensions of thinking and cognitive instruction* (pp. 15–51). Hillsdale, NJ: Erlbaum.

Queensland Department of Education. (1991). *Years 1–10 English language arts: Assessment guide.* Brisbane, Australia: Author.

Raphael, T.E., & Englert, C.S. (1990). Reading and writing: Partners in constructing meaning. *The Reading Teacher, 43*, 380–400.

Sadler, D.R. (1989). Formative assessment and the design of instructional systems. *Instructional Science, 18*, 119–144.

South Australian Department of Education. (1991). *Literacy assessment in practice: R–7 language arts.* Adelaide, Australia: Author.

Tierney, R.J., Carter, M.A., & Desai, L.E. (1991). *Portfolio assessment in the reading–writing classroom.* Norwood, MA: Christopher Gordon.

Valencia, S.W., Au, K.H., Scheu, J.A., & Kawakami, A.J. (1990). Assessment of students' ownership of literacy. *The Reading Teacher, 44*, 154–156.

van Kraayenoord, C.E., & Paris, S.G. (1992). Portfolio assessment: Its place in the Australian classroom. *Australian Journal of Language and Literacy, 15*, 93–104.

Weeks, B., & Leaker, J. (1991). *Managing literacy assessment with young learners.* Adelaide, Australia: ERA.

Wiggins G. (1992). On performance assessment: A conversation with Grant Wiggins. *Educational Leadership, 49*, 35–37.

Literacy assessment of students from poor and diverse communities: Changing the programs, changing the outcomes

Lynne Badger and Lyn Wilkinson

This article reports on the concerns and issues about literacy assessment that a small group of selected teachers who work in disadvantaged primary schools are grappling with in the everyday world of their classrooms.

One of the fundamental issues which confronts them is that cohorts of students from poor and disadvantaged communities perform less well on school literacy tasks than do students from more affluent families (Connell, 1992; Freebody & Ludwig, 1995; South Australian Department of Education, 1992; Williams, 1987). A major function of schools, it is often argued, is to sort and classify students, to discriminate among them, and to determine what kinds of socio-economic opportunities will be open to them. Assessment is one way in which schools do this. Because it acts as a gatekeeping mechanism, assessment is therefore heavily implicated in the production and maintenance of socio-cultural privilege (Connell, 1992, p. 20).

This constructs a dilemma for teachers in disadvantaged schools who are mediating between the diverse values and literacy practices of the groups of students they teach and the particular values and literacy practices which are privileged by mainstream curricula and assessment.

About the research project

This project focussed on the questions and concerns that the teachers in the research schools raised about the interrelationship of school literacy programs and assessment outcomes for students from poor and diverse communities. It was felt that these questions and concerns could provide insight for other practitioners in disadvantaged schools. Thus our aim as literacy educators was to explore and document the ways this group of teachers

From *The Australian Journal of Language and Literacy*, 21(2), June 1998. Reprinted with permission of the Australian Literacy Educators' Association.

conceptualised their role in promoting students' literacy performance and achieving more equitable literacy outcomes.

The documentation was part of a larger literacy research project conducted in a number of disadvantaged schools across metropolitan Adelaide, South Australia. These schools are designated as disadvantaged because they have large numbers of students whose families are receiving government assistance. The research team had won a grant from the Committee for the Advancement of University Teaching (CAUT) to produce three videos and accompanying written materials which explored the relationship between literacy, poverty, and schooling. It was our belief that the teacher development materials could be used to trigger conversations between other practitioners as they in turn explored this relationship in their own schools and classrooms. Thus we assumed that these materials would generate more genuine dialogue and have greater credibility for teachers and student teachers if they were grounded in the actual practices and concerns of other practitioners.

The research for the video which dealt specifically with literacy assessment was carried out with teachers working in classes from Reception (Kindergarten) to Year 7, the final year of primary schooling in South Australia. Early in the project the teachers simply wanted to know what we wished to see in their classrooms and what we would film. We explained the kinds of ideas we had and some of the issues that concerned us. As we worked with the teachers we observed and heard the interesting and challenging assessment practices that they talked about and that they were putting into practice. But rather than provide exemplars of "good assessment practice" we wanted the materials to foreground what was problematic from the viewpoint of teachers and other educators with a commitment to achieving more equitable literacy outcomes for students in disadvantaged schools. We also wanted to situate the classroom footage within a framework which explored the politics of advantage (Eveline, 1994) and structural inequality (Connell, 1992) within our society.

As we discussed this framing with teachers they not only began to respond to the questions we asked about their literacy assessment practices but also to the issues of equity we raised. In doing so they began to see themselves as co-enquirers rather than simply informants. Moreover, as we spent time in classrooms observing and interacting with students and sometimes their parents, as well as getting a "feel" for each classroom community, our discussions with the teachers became increasingly *dialogic* (Shor, 1980, pp. 95–96). That is, we acted as equals engaged in joint research rather than doing research *on* teachers and teaching, and this in turn allowed the teachers to have a significant measure of control. While we, the teacher educators, still formulated the actual framework for the research, in other respects there was genuine participation by our classroom colleagues. In particular, we worked in ways that incorporated their experiences, classroom practice, values, and beliefs, and which encouraged joint decision making about what aspects of their practical and intellectual work should be documented.

The interrelatedness of the classroom literacy program and assessment

Together we explored issues such as how students *at risk* are defined; how each classroom literacy practice privileges some students' knowledge and experiences and marginalises others; the cultural values associated with particular kinds of literacy and certain categories of texts; and how unexamined values and beliefs can unwittingly influence teaching practice in ways that contribute to students' literacy success or failure.

These issues may appear to go beyond the usual discussions of literacy assessment which tend to focus more on changing assessment techniques or developing better, different, or more technically advanced instruments. However, we believed that assessment and assessment techniques cannot be understood outside of what counts in the literacy program, and how this is shaped by what is valued and what counts as mainstream literacy practices and competencies. Such practices and competencies are socially and culturally constructed, which means that assessment of students' literacy competencies is an act of social judgement which has social consequences (Connell, 1993).

Because it is an act of social judgment, assessment of itself never provides a level playing field. No assessment tool is free of bias (Connell, 1992, p. 22). It is a myth that any assessment tool, and this includes standardised tests, teacher-devised assessments, and new approaches such as portfolios, can be objective in the sense that it is unbiassed or value-free. The kinds of tasks and questions that are set, the knowledge that is called on, the processes which students are required to undertake, all privilege some students' knowledge, experience, and practices over others. Teachers in disadvantaged schools have to "consider the extent to which assessment methods distort or reflect the literacy development of students from diverse backgrounds" (Garcia & Pearson, 1991, p. 254).

Thus a recurring feature of the dialogue we had with teachers was their focus on the literacy program. We found it impossible to talk about assessment without constantly coming back to issues of programming. It seemed that the literacy program was the most significant factor in making a difference to students' achievement. The two—the classroom literacy program and assessment of students' achievements—were inextricably linked. In other words, we found that teachers' literacy programs construct the limits and possibilities for students' school literacy performance, which is then the focus for assessment.

The teachers with whom we worked were grappling with the need to radically rethink the literacy programs they had offered to students, and were asking themselves the kinds of questions below.

What does my classroom program make possible?

What competencies are the students able to display?

What competencies are excluded by my program?

Which literacy practices and texts are privileged, and which marginalised by the program I offer?

While part of this rethinking meant reviewing assessment practices, it was clear that making a difference for students in disadvantaged schools is not simply a matter of changing or improving assessment techniques. More equitable outcomes result from literacy programs which reflect, build on, and assess a diversity of literacy practices.

The teachers were also grappling with the way in which assessment permeated their literacy programs. Students' literacy competence was assessed moment by moment throughout every school day, as teachers listened to them speak, heard them read aloud, observed them during writing and silent reading sessions, and interacted with them. From the moment that students entered the classroom, the "production of differences in literate competence begins" (Baker & Freebody, 1993, p. 291). Often subconsciously, teachers begin a mental ledger on each student, entering credits and debits according to how well the student matches up with their expectations about what counts as literate behaviour. This crediting is communicated to students both overtly and covertly, consciously and unconsciously, when teachers respond to their literacy work and behaviour. As Baker and Freebody point out, "[t]eachers do not rely on formal tests to infer how good children are at literacy; they hear this competence minute by minute in exchanges" (1993, p. 287).

The teachers in the project recognised assessment as a pervasive fact of classroom life. One teacher explained her viewpoint as follows.

I guess assessment goes on in a variety of situations in our classrooms. It is not just contained in language sessions where I go around and collect specific information but most of the assessment is actually found in real life experiences where [students] are writing letters of real importance like last year writing to get donations of food for camps...or class meeting agendas where children fill in the problems and concerns or issues they want to discuss in class meetings. Some children filled in SACON forms [minor works request forms]...and it really shows their power of language and how they can use it to get things done. So language assessment is done all day in a whole range of ways.

If teachers are to make a difference for students from disadvantaged groups, then they need to examine assessment in all its manifestations. Students' success and failure in literacy is not just measured at "transition points" such as the end of the term or the year, or the end of secondary school. It is constructed moment by moment as students engage in the literacy events offered by the teacher's program and as the teacher assesses their competence during these events.

Broadening opportunities for assessing students' literacy competencies

During the project both teachers and researchers have been challenged to take apart what has been naturalised, what is unexamined and assumed, to see how both programs and assessment practices are implicated in the reproduction of disadvantage. In interrogating their programs to achieve more equitable outcomes for students from poor and diverse communities, teachers identified three key interrelated aspects that need to be addressed. These aspects are:

- the diversity of literacy practices which are reflected in the program,
- the constraints and possibilities of classroom literacy practices, and
- student perspectives.

Diversity of literacy practices reflected in the program

Teachers who are concerned about equity place "social justice at the foundation of thinking about curriculum and assessment" (Connell, 1993, p. 83). This leads them to consider the ways in which their programs reflect or fail to reflect the diversity of literacy practice in the wider community. The traditional school literacy curriculum has privileged the practices, texts, content, and forms (Connell, 1992, p. 22) of some groups in the community over others, giving advantage to the children from these groups. If this is to be redressed then researchers and teachers need to:

look at the different kinds of literacy practices that go on in different sub-cultures and in different areas and in different workspaces and to look at different kinds of ways in which they are projected back into schooling—to look at the way in which the activities that go on in the classroom reflect or fail to reflect certain sorts of ways in which reading and writing are routinely practised in the everyday lives of people in different sectors of the society, different work sectors, different domestic sectors, different kinds of communities. (Peter Freebody, video transcript in Badger et al., 1997)

The teachers in the project were, to varying extents, trying to broaden the range of literacy practices and texts offered in their classrooms. They realised that the diversity of students' experiences means that they bring to school different strengths and competencies in literacy, many of which are unrecognised and unvalued in the traditional literacy curriculum. For example, in one school, nine- and ten-year-old students were extremely competent in using timetables to travel to a seaside suburb where there is considerable weekend entertainment, adeptly making connections between two buses and a tram. When the teachers recognised the students possessed such skills they were able to credit them and build on them in their classroom literacy programs.

In the same school, teachers saw how other areas of the curriculum offered opportunity for different literacy practices. For example, the students grew vegetables, and as part of that endeavour they read seed packets, brochures, and instructions about planting and caring for the plants as well as for dealing with weeds and pests. They wrote labels for different vegetables, and kept descriptive logs recording the growth (or death!) of their plants. Again, many of the students sang in the school choir, where there were opportunities for them to share their interpretations of lyrics, as well as to discuss the meanings of obscure or unfamiliar words.

In another school, two of the junior primary teachers had a particular interest in understanding the nexus between the practices which counted in their literacy programs, the range of outcomes which their programs made possible and the ways they assessed their students' literacy competencies. These teachers too were involved in an on-going process of modifying the curriculum they offered so as to include opportunities for students to use literacies beyond the usual school literacies. They had a particular focus on using literacy for social action. For instance, the students were involved in writing letters to cereal manufacturing companies to request their support in providing breakfast foods for the school camp because the school community did not have the material resources to meet all the costs required to send students to the camp.

In this same classroom students regularly filled out the forms through which schools request minor works and repairs. When students identified that repairs were needed to school property they obtained and completed the form. To do this successfully they had to make a range of decisions about the location of the problem and the category of repair needed, providing accurate information that could be acted on by the maintenance workers when they came to the site. Those who filled out the form also had responsibility for faxing it to the appropriate authority. The students who had been in the school for some time took this responsibility seriously for themselves, and also inducted new students into the processes.

Additionally, students used the literacy practices involved in democratic decision making. Those with designated executive responsibility regularly ran class meetings where the class responded to items that students placed on the agenda, writing minutes to provide a record of decisions that they could refer to later.

These same teachers worked with students to identify a range of classroom responsibilities (e.g., lunch monitors) and developed position descriptions for them. Individual students then selected a position of interest to them and applied for it in writing, arguing their suitability against the criteria, and providing a reference from a family member or friend. The application was read by a selection committee of peers who made the decision as to which applicant got the position. All the positions were vacated at the end of each term and the process was repeated.

The kinds of literacy events described above are very different from the traditional school literacy tasks which focus on instruction or evaluation. Through these and many other literacy events the teachers provided a variety of opportunities for students to learn and to demonstrate their literacy competencies, usually through tasks that were real and meaningful for them.

Constraints and possibilities of classroom literacy practices

There is more to constructing an inclusive curriculum, however, than simply providing a diversity of literacy events. Literacy events in themselves are not socially or culturally neutral, but may be enacted in a variety of ways depending on the rules for the discourse within particular communities. Therefore literacy events themselves have to provide spaces for students to participate in ways that take cognisance of students' known ways of behaving and which allow them to build on and extend their understandings. Haas Dyson highlights this point when she says, "If a curriculum is to be truly responsive to diversity, truly child-centred, it must be permeable enough to allow for children's ways of participating in school literacy events" (Haas Dyson, 1992, p. 41).

Teachers in the project understood the need to attend to the ways in which different groups of students participated in and were positioned by specific literacy events. This led them to reflect on and try to understand different students' perspectives on and participation in the events.

One teacher explained how this presented her with a major challenge:

> One of the biggest challenges I face in teaching in a disadvantaged school is...constantly questioning what I present to children. So when I'm presenting something to children I examine the impact that it's going to have on them. For example, when I'm presenting a book to children I try to look at it through each individual child's eyes and ask what messages will this give Aboriginal children in my class. What messages will it give the non-English-speaking background children?

The quote demonstrates one of the ways in which the teachers tried to make their teaching more inclusive of a diverse range of students' experiences, serving to render the "socio–educational barriers more permeable" (Connell, Johnston, & White, 1994, p. 211). They sought to understand how students might interpret the classroom literacy events in which they participated (Garcia & Pearson, 1991) and how these events have the potential to both constrain and to enable different groups of students in the class. Two examples from the classroom demonstrate how teachers analysed literacy practices.

One Year 7 teacher came to understand the difficulties and hurdles she had unwittingly constructed when she demanded that during silent reading time students read only novels. She saw that many of the students were selecting familiar formula novel series such as *Sweet Valley High*, *Goosebumps*, *Hair Raisers*, and *Babysitters Club*, or they were only "pretending" to read the book in front of them. She realised that she had been privileging the reading of novels and negating a body of texts which students found interesting and enjoyable, thus limiting the range of texts on which students could develop and demonstrate their reading competencies. She has now changed her practice and permits the reading of magazines and comics during silent reading time.

A junior primary teacher questioned the valorisation of class meetings as a means of allowing students to experience democratic decision making. Her analysis of these meetings helped her to understand that the usual procedures are based on a "white middle class model of operating" which serves to marginalise Aboriginal students in particular.

Sometimes we provide situations in schools where we are actually limiting the information we obtain about students. For example, we have class meetings...which are set up on a white middle class model. We have one person talking at a time, people put their hands up and people vote. This can actually limit the involvement of some of the cultural groups we have in our school. For example Aboriginal children often don't work well on that model, don't work well in that kind of a situation. So even though it is important they are exposed to different situations we really need to incorporate some of the ways that they learn and talk in our class meetings. So we may set up lots of situations where children can come up with ideas in small groups and then have the opportunity to share those back with the class in a class meeting rather than just use the one model.

Rather than assess the students as unable to participate, as inadequate, or as lacking in confidence, this teacher analysed the practice from students' perspectives and modified it to provide a means for all the students to participate. In this way she avoided "reading" the limitations of the practice as limitations of the students. Students cannot receive credit for the literacy understandings and skills they have if the program fails to give them opportunities to show what they know and can do.

Students' perspectives

If a literacy program is to be equitable it needs to reflect the diversity of students' literacy practices, world views, and experiences. In addition, teachers need to find out how students are responding to the program that is being offered to them. It is argued that "[t]o understand...children's perspectives in school is to gain some insight into how they make sense of and interpret instructional experiences" (Dahl, 1995, p. 1). Understanding students' perspectives—what they are taking from the literacy program, their sense of success and failure, their goals and expectations—is important for teachers modifying and adapting the program.

In traditional forms of assessment, the knowledge that "counts" about students' achievement has been predominantly based on the teacher's perceptions. Student knowledge of who they are as literacy users and their literacy achievements has been completely discounted. The teachers in the research project were actively working to redress this, and to include students' perspectives as part of the data which informed their assessment processes and their program evaluation.

The change from student as object of assessment (Edelsky, 1991, p. 87) to student as participant in assessment takes account of the constructed nature of knowledge. If we accept that knowledge is constructed, then the knower is an intimate part of the known (Johnston, 1989), and their perspective should be made to count.

In the same way that classroom programs need to accommodate the multiplicity of literacy experiences, assessment practices have to explore the multiplicity of perceptions (Taylor, 1990) which are reflected in classrooms serving diverse communities.

> To assert privilege for one type of voice among all others in a classroom promotes and maintains a hierarchy based on nationality, gender, race, economic class, and ethnicity. Unless teachers and students are allowed and willing to listen to each other...to use their multiplicity of voices in any classroom, there is little hope for democratic development in our society. (Shannon, 1993, p. 92)

Teachers in the project schools were clear that this sentiment must extend to assessment, given its predominance in shaping the curriculum. Student self-assessment can serve to change the power dimension in classrooms, affirming students as one of the major stakeholders in the assessment process.

While self-assessment is seen to be empowering for students, it is not unproblematic. It cannot be accepted uncritically as a quick route to equity-based assessment. It can be as subject to bias and constraint as other kinds of assessment, with students "locked into seeing things only through the single set of lenses provided for them by their cultural guardians" (O'Loughlin, 1995, p. 107). When students wrote comments such as:

- I can write lots of genres
- I can write neatly with finger spaces between my words
- I'm a good reader because I borrow lots of fiction from the library

project teachers reviewed their programs in the light of the emphases and values on which students were focusing.

Interviews with students revealed that some of the kinds of self-assessment required were difficult. They said that parents and caregivers were likely to ask more questions than previously about their literacy achievement, and that they were expected to be able to give reasons and explanations in a way that they hadn't in the past. They had to take responsibility for their learning, and be able to justify their judgements about their work, and they told us that this was not easy to do.

> I think that the hardest part on the sheet is "How did I go?" because it's really hard to write about yourself because when you show your teacher or your parents at the interview they read it and then you get home and

they talk to you about it and it's really hard to talk about yourself and write about yourself. (Kate, Year 7)

When students' perceptions count as a source of information, and teachers understand the complexity of how these perceptions are constructed in the classroom, then they are in a better position to understand the relationship between their programs and students' literacy outcomes.

Conclusion

It can be argued that the whole enterprise of changing literacy outcomes for students from diverse and poor communities is less about finding more technically efficient assessment tools and more about changing classroom literacy programs. As teaching and assessment are inextricably linked, teachers' programs have to provide the spaces and opportunities through which students can demonstrate the diversity of their literacy competencies and build on those to use literacy as a powerful tool for "shaping identity, knowledge and power" (Luke, 1993, p. 48).

REFERENCES

Badger, L., Wilkinson, L., Comber, B., Nixon, H., & Hill, S. (1997). *Literacy assessment in disadvantaged schools*, Video module 6. Melbourne: Eleanor Curtain.

Baker, C., & Freebody, P. (1993). The crediting of literate competence in classroom talk. *The Australian Journal of Language and Literacy, 16*(4), 279–294.

Connell, R. (1992). Measuring up: Assessment, evaluation and educational disadvantage. *ACSA Teaching Resource No. 2*, Belconnen, ACT: Australian Curriculum Studies Association.

Connell, R. (1993). *Schools and social justice*. Toronto: Our Schools/Our Selves Production.

Connell, R., Johnston, K., & White, V. (1994). The issue of poverty and educational measurement. In E. Hatton (Ed.), *Understanding teaching: Curriculum and the social context of schooling*. Sydney: Harcourt Brace.

Dahl, K. (1995). Challenges in understanding the learner's perspective. *Theory Into Practice, 34*(2), 1, 124–130.

Haas Dyson, A. (1992). The case of the singing scientist: A performance perspective on the 'stages' of school literacy. *Written Communication, 9*(1), 3–47.

Edelsky, C. (1991). *With literacy and social justice for all: Rethinking the social in language and education*. London: Falmer Press.

Eveline, J. (1994, Autumn). The politics of advantage. *Australian Feminist Studies, 19*, 129–154.

Freebody, P., & Ludwig, C. (1995). *Everyday literate practices in and out of schools in low socio-economic urban communities: Executive summary*. Canberra: Department of Education, Employment and Training; Melbourne: Curriculum Corporation.

Garcia, G., & Pearson, P. (1991). The role of assessment in a diverse society. In E. Hiebert (Ed.), *Literacy for a diverse society*. New York: Teachers College Press.

Johnston, P. (1989). Constructive evaluation and the improvement of teaching and learning. *Teachers College Record, 90*(4), 509–528.

Luke, A. (1993). The social construction of literacy in the primary school. In L. Unsworth (Ed.), *Literacy learning and teaching: Language as social practice in the primary school*. Melbourne: Macmillan.

O'Loughlin, M. (1995). Daring the imagination: Unlocking voices of dissent and possibility in teaching. *Theory Into Practice, 34*(2), 107–116.

Shannon, P. (1993). Developing democratic voices. *The Reading Teacher, 47*, 86–94.

Shor, I. (1980). *Critical teaching and everyday life*. Boston: South End Press.

South Australian Department of Education. (1992). *Writing reading assessment programme: Final report*. Adelaide: Author.

Taylor, D. (1990). Teaching without testing: Assessing the complexity of children's literacy learning. *English Education, 22*(1), 4–74.

Williams, T. (1987). *Participation in education* (Research Monograph No. 30). Hawthorn, Victoria: Australian Council for Education Research.

Assessment: Profiling literacy with young Indigenous children

Jenni Connor

Those receiving funds under the Commonwealth Indigenous Education Strategic Initiatives Program (IESIP) are required to report each year on the progress in Literacy and Numeracy of Indigenous children enrolled in their kindergarten/preschool/child care centres.

During the monitoring and reporting processes in recent years, it has become apparent that a number of educational centres have found it difficult to assess the competence of their children, especially as it related to preparing them for school.

In 2000, the then Department of Education, Training and Youth Affairs (DETYA) (now DEST) convened a Steering Committee with broad representation from State and Territory government and independent authorities. The Committee was to advise on a Framework for assessing young children's literacy learning that would provide consistency of reporting criteria, be inclusive of Indigenous literacy learning and be supportive of early years practitioners in their work with young children.

The Committee was assisted by two experts in Early Childhood Education—Professor Bridie Raban, Mooroolbeck Chair of Early Childhood, University of Melbourne, and Dr. Marilyn Fleer, then Associate Professor in Education at University of Canberra—both of whom had been Research Fellows with DETYA. (Dr. Fleer is now Professor of Early Childhood at Monash University.)

The Committee commenced by examining the range of early assessment screening frameworks used across the nation, to identify common ground and items applicable to varying learning contexts for Indigenous children.

As a result of the Committee's work, a Preschool Profile and teachers' guide were developed. The Profile focuses on key "understandings" that children gain from their families, communities, and early learning settings that are crucial to later literacy and numeracy success. The Profile is based on a socio-cultural assessment paradigm, using the work of Bruner and

From *Practically Primary*, 7(2), June 2002. Reprinted with permission of the Australian Literacy Educators' Association.

Vygotsky. It therefore seeks to "map the interactions" between novice (young child) and experienced (adult or older peers) learners and their move from "Modelled," through "Shared" to "Independent" demonstration of understandings, for both literacy and numeracy.

The Profile was piloted in Tasmania, Victoria, Western Australia, and Queensland in remote, rural, and urban settings with students from diverse language backgrounds.

Professor Patrick Griffin, from Melbourne University analysed the completed profiles of 385 children and reported on the reliability and validity of the Profile as an assessment instrument.

Figure 1. Sample of the profile items

Profile of print literacy awareness and understanding

		With adult/peer support and minimal child input (modelled)	Jointly undertaken by child and adult/peer (shared)	Child takes leadership and/or works independently (independent)
Shows awareness of the print literacy they see in their home	In language of instruction			
	In English			
Shows awareness of the print literacy they see in their community	In language of instruction			
	In English			
Shows awareness that printed texts vary according to purpose	In language of instruction			
	In English			
Shows understanding of the link between experience and written text	In language of instruction			
	In English			
Knows that texts are "read" from left to right and from top to bottom of the lines	In language of instruction			
	In English			
Can recognise own name	In language of instruction			
	In English			

Figure 2. Table showing baseline estimates for different groups of children

Variables	Category	Achieving independence on all descriptors		Not achieving independence on all descriptors		Total
		%	N	%	N	N
Indigenous	Indigenous	46.0	64	54.0	75	139
	Non–Indigenous	55.2	113	44.7	102	215
	Total		177		177	354
Gender	Female	52.6	92	47.4	83	175
	Male	47.1	85	52.9	95	180
	Total		177		178	355
Context	Remote	48.4	15	51.6	16	31
	Rural	43.4	56	56.6	73	129
	Urban	54.2	104	45.8	88	192
	Total		175		177	352
Home language	English	50.5	170	49.5	167	337
	Other language	33.3	5	66.7	10	15
	Total		175		177	352
Age	< 4.10 y	45.9	22	54.1	26	48
	4.10–5.7 y	47.1	100	52.9	112	212
	> 5.7 y	65.2	62	34.8	33	95
	Total		184		171	355

The trial yielded some interesting data:

- 46% of Indigenous children were "Independent" on all measures,
- there were minimal differences when analysed by gender,
- urban children were marginally, but not significantly more successful,
- the greatest differences were related to age and to Language Backgrounds Other Than English, and
- the most challenging items were those involving concepts about how written symbols retain constant meaning.

What is remarkable about this display of results, is the almost equal numbers of children in this pilot sample who achieved independence on all descriptors and those who did not. The direction of any trend towards those children who were deemed by their teachers to be most advanced, were identified as those who were older and those who spoke English at home.

(Table and quotation from: *Preschool Profile, DETYA Indigenous Education Branch, Final Report of Pilot Survey.* Professor Bridie Raban, Professor Patrick Griffin.)

Naturally, these results need careful interpretation. The trial was relatively small and it is unwise to extrapolate too generally. It is not surprising that success on these criteria increases with maturity and learning experience, or that having to "switch" between the requirements of two language systems might impact on early progress. However, it seems significant that many Indigenous children perform creditably on measures in preschool, at age four and five, while nationally, Indigenous children's achievement on Benchmarks a few years later is significantly below their non-Indigenous peers.

A number of factors may impinge on this phenomenon, including exacerbated health problems, increasing mobility, and changing family circumstances. It is also likely that there are strong connections between home, culture, and centre in the preschool years, adult—child ratios may be lower, and a play-based, collaborative learning program is conducive to the learning of young Indigenous children. In addition, the pilot results beg the question of "what is measured/what is valued?": *If the IESIP Profile strives to value and build on what children already know, understand, and can do as a result of learning in their communities, do our later assessment practices similarly respect prior learning and cultural knowledge?*

In 2001, DETYA arranged a trial implementation of the Profile with Independent Preschool providers in Queensland, New South Wales, South Australia, and Western Australia. Workshops were conducted in regional centres such as Cairns, Mildura, Dubbo, Lismore, and Broome and participants also travelled to Sydney, Brisbane, Perth, and Melbourne. Indigenous teacher assistants were usually present at all meetings and Indigenous community members often attended regional workshops.

Profile not a checklist

The Profile is not a checklist. It relies on teachers' capacity to make sound, informed, professional judgements about children's learning. Within the early years teaching community, there is a wide range of training and experience and, especially between Independent centres, limited opportunity for professional exchange and "moderation."

The workshops therefore intended to familiarise participants with the profile and its use, build networks of professional support between independent and often isolated practitioners, and to uncover with the educators what they knew about children's understandings, and what their children knew, that they so far might not have realised.

The workshop model was based on the following structure:

- from practice into theory
- personalising the profile—revealing what teachers know and already do
- generalising from different contexts—"what does this example demonstrate understanding about?"
- revealing and valuing cultural and community literacy and numeracy knowledge—literacy as social practice!
- building networks of support and consistent bases for judgement.

Some of the "lessons" from the implementation included:

- Literacy is not just found in hardcover narrative—literacy is signs, tracks, symbols, songs and stories, graffiti, cards, video packs, TV guides, Nintendo, catalogues, letters, bills....
- Numeracy isn't "just numbers and measuring tapes"—numeracy is "river high/river low," "my mob bigger than your mob," mustering, fishing, bush trips, darts, bingo, speed signs, kinship, families....

BUT, as community members said to us: *"You fellas don't count our stuff."*

These examples show just how contextual "knowledge" is. The contexts change—from the fishing village of Strahan in Tasmania, to the desert in the West—the principle remains the same: *"what is the child demonstrating understanding about?"*

We now have a wealth of information about "what works" to improve outcomes for Indigenous learners. From researchers such as Professor Paul Hughes from Flinders University and others, we have principles for success such as:

- belief in success,
- clear targets and monitoring,
- adequate resources,
- a rich teaching repertoire to match learners' needs and to make literacy learning explicit,
- family support, including support for regular attendance,
- a Curriculum that builds on student knowledge, and
- coordinated cross-agency support.

From projects such as the AECA (Australian Early Childhood Association)-managed Building Bridges, we know that families recognise and value what their children know—we just have to find the time and the ways to ask them.

My own conclusions are simple, if difficult to implement:

- expectations tailor results—we get what we expect from all children
- learning drives development—we can't afford to wait
- adult modelling and interaction reveals children's emerging understandings—which indicate program goals
- we must work from context to concept—using settings, materials, and purposes that make sense to young learners
- assessment reveals what we value—we need new measures and "new eyes" to note the important things young children understand

Using running records in the classroom

Lorraine Wilson and Melissa Dash

> There are many people who believe that simply counting errors on in-formal reading inventories can help a teacher determine a student's in-structional level. (Geeslin, 1972)

It is over thirty years since the work of Ken and Yetta Goodman showed that miscues are a natural part of the reading process. What is good or bad about a reading miscue (oral reading error) is the extent to which that miscue contributes to or interferes with the ongoing meaning–making process. Therefore, in assessing a child's running record, the percentage of correct words is not the issue, but rather each miscue needs to be analysed. For each miscue we need to ask:

- Did the word make sense in the context?
- Why did the child say this?
- Has syntactic or semantic knowledge contributed to the miscue?
- Has graphophonic knowledge contributed?
- Was there a self-correction? Why/why not?
- Was the self correction necessary for meaning?

The value of running records is that they provide teachers with infor-mation about the child's use of the cuing systems—graphophonic, syntac-tic, and semantic. By analysing this information a teacher builds up a picture of a child's reading behaviours—both strengths and weaknesses—so that a range of strategies can be developed to assist her to become a more profi-cient and independent reader.

A running record of the reading of eight year old Sean

Sean read *Winni Allfours* by Babbette Cole and a running record was taken. For this text Sean had a 1:14 error rate, that is, he read with 93% word

From "From the Classroom," *Practically Primary*, 4(1), February 1999. Reprinted with permission of the Australian Literacy Educators' Association.

accuracy. His self correction ratio was 1:5. But these statistics do not provide us with a picture of Sean as a reader.

An analysis of Sean's miscues, that is, his deviation from the literal text, allows us to determine which cueing systems and reading strategies he used as he read. This analysis then informs teaching.

/   /   **allow (O)** /   /   /   /

/   / **(R) want to** / /   /   /

We don't / approve of people who own ponies. **(R)**

——————————————————————————/

In his first reading of this sentence Sean used the following strategies: he repeated a word (possibly to gain time for the difficult words following), substituted two words for one, and read on. Then he re-read the whole sentence, substituted "allow" for "approve," and omitted "of" to make a syntactically correct sentence where meaning was maintained.

The next section of text shows Sean using a range of strategies and drawing upon different cueing systems:

/ / / /   / /   **said**   /   /

"What are we going to do?" shrieked her Mum

she   /   / **(P)(R)** **(O)**   /   /

"She's ruined the /   organic vegetable patch!"

/   /   /   /   /

"Serves them right" said Winni

Three errors were recorded for this section, but meaning has not been lost. When Sean came across an unfamiliar word "organic" he used graphophonic information to identify the initial letter-sound, then referred to the illustrations to see which objects began with "o." He seemed puzzled when he could not find a word that made sense in the context, so he then tried a different strategy, re-reading the whole sentence and omitting the difficult word.

In the following sentence Sean substituted a semantically acceptable word for "beat" and over-generalised the past tense ending. Once again meaning is maintained.

/ / **breaked** / /   /

But they beat the world record.

Sean gave a detailed retelling of the text outlining the main characters and the sequence of events in the text. He understood the meaning of the story. In the context of an authentic literacy event—reading an interesting book—the running record gave his teacher, Melissa, valuable information about his development as a reader.

Conclusion

As Yetta Goodman wrote in 1997, reviewing twenty-five years of miscue analysis:

> Miscue analysis is exciting...the reader gives evidence about the degree to which what he is reading makes sense to him. To simply count miscues is to short-circuit a complex reading process. Quick judgments regarding readers can be harmful and lead to mistaken judgments though they appear to provide an easy way of classifying a student's reading ability.

REFERENCES

Cole, B. (1995). *Winni Allfours.* London: Penguin, Picture Puffin.

Geeslin, R., (1972). The placement inventory alternative. *The Reading Teacher, 25,* 332–335.

Goodman, Y. (1997). Reading diagnosis—qualitative or quantitative? *The Reading Teacher, 50,* 534–538.

Authentic assessment
and system accountability

Anne Nelson

System accountability has assumed prime importance in the last ten years, right across Australia. Most states use some sort of "basic skills" testing as well as curriculum outcome statements against which student progress is measured.

In Victoria, schools are expected to structure their teaching around the Curriculum and Standards Framework (CSF), which was derived from the eight National Profiles.

CSF Levels are tied to particular age-grade expectations: Level 1 is the end of Prep, Level 2 the end of Grade 2, and so on. Each child's progress must be reported as "Beginning," "Consolidating," or "Established" within the relevant Level.

As there are four primary levels, each Victorian child might progress through 12 reporting levels in seven years—from "Beginning Level 1" to "Established Level 4." These reports are made in Mathematics, English, and Science.

Victorian schools are required to list the CSF level and sub-level of all children in their Annual Reports. In the midst of all this grading and levelling it would be easy to surrender authentic practices and just tick the boxes on a report form.

Assessing reading in an authentic way

Anne uses running records several times a term for all children, and more often for those in difficulty or at risk. These are noted on her own running record proforma and kept in a folder.

During guided reading sessions she writes observational notes and sometimes takes informal running records. These observations also record the children's attitudes, engagement, and enjoyment in the task.

From "From the Classroom," *Practically Primary*, 4(1), February 1999. Reprinted with permission of the Australian Literacy Educators' Association.

Periodically the class has a special performance called "Guest Reader," in which children take turns to read rehearsed text to the others, while Anne takes notes on a guest reader proforma.

Anne's children participate in cross-age tutoring three times a week: "Tutors are trained to note important features of their tutee's reading. They record their comments on a proforma that they helped design."

Anne includes these tutor comments in her own assessment process.

Each child has their own small box of books from which they choose their own book to take home each day.

Teachers at Spensley St. have sorted the home reading books according to broad bands of levelled text, but allow children to borrow outside their supposed level, as their interests dictate. Also in the box is a communication book (an exercise book cut in half). The parent writes the date, title, and a brief comment whenever the child takes a book home to read. Sometimes children write their own evaluative comments in here too.

Anne: "I regularly write comments about the child's reading in here too, because it's part of my reporting process."

Thus Anne has extensive written data to draw on when assessing a child's reading progress, ranging from informal notes to a bank of running records.

Anne's assessment is essentially qualitative, rather than a quantitative measurement:

> I don't calculate the percentage of errors. I really use them (the running records) for two reasons. One is to check that the child is choosing and reading books at an appropriate level.... I encourage them to balance reading in a comfortable way with taking a challenge. Second I look at the kinds of miscues to see the areas that need work and I note their strengths or gains.

Reporting to parents

This accumulated assessment data helps Anne make "on balance judgments" about each child, which she summarises on the school's Report Form. The reading descriptors for Levels 1, 2, and 3 are shown here (that is, the Victorian expectations for Prep to Grade 4).

The school does not refer to this report as a "profile" but its characteristics are comparable to the National Profile for English, only shorter and more manageable for parents.

Anne explains: "We have developed 'menus' from the CSF, using the Curriculum Focus Statements for each level and incorporating First Steps

CSF Level 1
Engages in reading–like behavior, e.g., holds book correctly, turns pages
Invents stories to accompany pictures, using story–like phrases from text
Shows awareness of letter/sound relationships
Recognises a number of works in text

CSF Level 2
Uses strategies for interpreting text, including self-correction
Uses own knowledge and experiences to link to a variety of texts
Reads for meaning, has comprehension strategies
Selects appropriate texts

CSF Level 3
Reflects on text, e.g., plot, characterization, main idea
Clarifies or corrects meaning by pausing, re–reading, and reading on
Can verbalise own reading strategies
Attempts to work out meaning of unknown words

indicators. We refer to the menus during our planning days when we set the outcomes to focus on for the next term."

Using these menus as a type of school-based profile, Spensley St. teachers show each child's reading development over time.

Key statements from the menu are listed on the Report Form for parents. There are similar statements for Writing, Speaking and Listening, and Mathematics. (Science has not been developed yet.)

"There's a difference between the larger 'menu' and the actual outcome statements we select at any given time. Development over time is shown by keeping some of the outcome statements the same from semester to semester. New statements are added and others dropped according to the topic or genre or focus we've studied."

Comprehensive reporting

This article concentrates on "Reading," but Anne's assessment of her children is comprehensive. With "Writing," for example, she uses:

- Work samples to position the child on the writing menu.
- "Research Books" in which each child reports on what she's learnt from the current integrated unit of work. Children put their books

together themselves, with teacher consultation. It shows spelling development, finished pieces, reading comprehension, even artwork. (This idea was adapted by Spensley St. teachers from an initiative of Heathcote Primary School, in country Victoria.)

- Projects, displayed around the room, often the result of group work.

- A class presentation for parents and other visitors, called "Ask the Expert" where children show and discuss projects or research (this activity also helps Anne gather data for assessing Listening and Speaking).

Self evaluations

Children at Spensley St. compile a "Self Evaluation Book," which is a student portfolio showing a few pieces of work from each term. Teachers and children jointly select English, Maths, and Integrated Unit samples, without teacher annotation. Many children, however, write evaluative comments for their work samples, for example, "I chose this work because it shows that I know about...."

These samples are discussed at parent teacher interview—children may attend their own interview—and the book is taken home at the end of the year, as a permanent record of work.

Two of Bethany's self evaluations in her end of year Self Evaluation Book

Formal self evaluations are included, in the form of learning logs. They are usually directed at the current unit of work. Sometimes children write more general self evaluations ("how I feel about reading/maths," etc.).

Meeting system requirements

When completed, the Student Progress Report is talked through at the parent–teacher interview. It's typically about eight pages long. The other records mentioned above, the Self-Evaluation Book, and the child's Research Book also inform the interview, and the child shows his or her projects and other work.

But very little of this rich array of data is required by the Victorian Department of Education. The system's requirement is simply that children be put onto a CSF Level, firstly for parent reporting, secondly for annual departmental reporting. Victorian schools are required to list the CSF Level of each and every child in an Annual School Report.

Because the outcome statements on the parent report form are labelled as "CSF Levels," the Victorian departmental requirements are easily met, without affecting the validity or authenticity of the extensive assessment practices.

Essentially, meeting these requirements is irrelevant and superfluous to the real purpose of the assessment—keeping track of kids in order to help them learn better.

All things in moderation: A whole school approach to authentic assessment

John Davidson

A t Moonee Ponds West Primary School, a lot of teacher effort goes into constructing valid assessment methods. The main assessment tool, developed over many years, is a form of **Cumulative File**, consisting of annotated work samples drawn from everyday classroom work. Additional data on a child's progress is compiled from extensive conference notes, often distilled or summarised as **Profiles**—one for reading, another for mathematics.

Because their source is actual classroom activity (not special data generated by one-off tests), these assessment methods are well grounded and any decisions made about a child's learning are based on real evidence.

The school has developed its own **Reading Profile**, used to map a child's development from Prep to Grade 6. The indicators on this profile are objective, observable behaviours such as "Recognises own name" or "Indicates 1:1 correspondence between printed and spoken word." They represent collective teacher beliefs about reading and are based mainly on tacit teacher knowledge, as well as published curriculum documents. For example, both the WA First Steps Reading Continuum and the National Profile have been referred to, both for their sequencing and as checks that all essential behaviours are covered. The Tasmanian Pathways document was used as a template for the patchwork-type layout.

This Reading Profile began in 1991 as a linear checklist of beginning and emergent reading behaviours. Over the years many teachers have helped refine and develop it into a set of interlocking descriptors, organised in broad, developmentally appropriate bands (not graded levels) covering the whole of primary school (and early secondary).

The linear layout gave way to more of a "jigsaw-like" pattern, because teachers know that children don't develop in simplistic straight lines. Reading development typically shows leaps, pauses, consolidation, even regression at times, and an authentic record of development has to allow for a child's idiosyncratic path.

From "From the Classroom," *Practically Primary*, 4(1), February 1999. Reprinted with permission of the Australian Literacy Educators' Association.

A section of the P–6 Reading Profile, used across the whole school

MPW—Prep to Six Reading Development Profile

NAME:

Recognises own name, friends' names Joins in familiar stories	Predicts story from cover	Invents story to accompany pictures Uses story-like/core phrases from text	Able to re-read some of own written language Recognises some familiar sight words
Makes links to own experience when listening or reading books		Knows print contains the message (e.g., directionality, conventions, story makes sense, etc.)	Recites text from memory with fluency and/or expression
Re-reads fluently after listening post, repeated, or shared reading		Uses semantics, memory, pictures, and sight words to approximate a known text	
Indicates when reading doesn't make sense Attempts self-correction to make sense		Uses illustrations to decode text Uses grapho-phonics (sound–letter information) to decode Uses semantics (sense of story) to decode	
Reads silently for longer periods		Recites text with accuracy, while focused on print	

The Profile summarises the raw data collected by teachers at reading conferences—every entry on a child's Profile can be backed up by conference notes, anecdotals, or work samples. It is used as both an assessment instrument and as a reporting tool for parents.

Like the Reading Profile, the school's system of **Cumulative Assessment Files** has been developed over many years, with input from all teachers at curriculum and team meetings, and at whole-day PD sessions. This system (called simply "Files" at Moonee West) originated in Victoria in the early 1970s, well before the "portfolio movement" got under way in the U.S. in the late 1980s.

Our files began life as a simple collection of work samples. Over the years, more teacher comment was added, along with contextual information, analysis, and most importantly, the child's own reflections and self-evaluations. They are not collections of "best work."

Some problems of holistic, authentic evaluation remain to be solved. For example, how can a "file" portray changes in playground behaviour? How do you show emerging social maturity or self-confidence? To some extent these questions are tackled through the child's own **self evaluations**, or with specific projects like writer's profiles. (See Jenny Hodges' and Merredith Hillebrand's article "Children's views of themselves as authors" in the February 1999 edition of *Practically Primary*.)

Standardised, summative, or multiple choice tests are not used at all at Moonee Ponds West. While moving away from standardisation, these teachers have developed their own form of **moderation** in order to ensure the authenticity of their assessments.

Before each reporting period (mid-year and end of year), teachers get together in their teams to compare a selection of their Assessment Files and Profiles. Each classroom teacher selects a child considered to be progressing "normally" and one considered to be "at risk." Other classroom teachers, who usually work with similar class structures, examine the work samples, profiles, and conference notes to see if they would have drawn conclusions similar to those of the assessing teacher.

Lots of talk ensues, with many suggestions and questions about the annotations and judgments to be made, for example:

- Has this child's proofreading improved over time?
- Does this or that class write across a range of genre?
- Are adequate science and technology samples included in the file?
- Do teachers use similar terminology in their conference notes?

Some teachers give written feedback to their colleagues, or use "post-it" sticky labels on the actual samples or profiles. The assessing teacher can then consider the range of comments later.

Many ideas are shared and innovations suggested. Teachers treat each other as professional equals during these meetings, but willingly risk their credibility by laying bare their views on learning, their written notes on children, and, by implication, their own teaching practice.

In the end, the unanimous view is that it's well worth the risk—words like "empowerment," "trust," "valid judgment" flow around the room, and the meetings run late into the evening. Personal and professional enhancement is a valuable by-product of this moderation process.

Since everyone is submitting files for moderation, consensus can be reached about what "normal progress" is, and what indicates a child is "at risk."

The criteria for these judgments are discussed by the teachers concerned, they're not imposed by test scores or lists of "outcomes" handed down from on high.

As well, the school gains confidence that the teachers have agreed on what is a reasonable expectation for each stage of learning, and that all teachers are using similar assessment tools. This means that the assessment documents themselves are dependable or trustworthy—they are reliable as well as valid.

Portfolios: Valuing the whole of children's learning

Jeff Wilson

> Assessment should relate to the goals of the curriculum and not deflect the teaching program from these goals. It should be shaped by and confirm the intentions of learning. Assessment should identify students' achievements and directions for further learning. (ACSA Policy, 1994)

Indeed it is the teachers' responsibility to make sure that the assessments carried out authenticate the learning of the students they teach. If assessment does not do this, then the methods of assessment are probably not authentic.

Portfolios or similar procedures have become the central assessment tool for many classroom teachers in many schools. They provide a flexible and authentic method of mapping the learning journeys in a classroom and are able to reflect the individuality of each child.

This article looks at the way portfolios are used at Albanvale Primary School.

What are portfolios?

The portfolios at Albanvale are a collection of children's work that show significant aspects of development throughout the year. The pieces have been collected at various stages of the learning process and therefore include drafts and work in progress, as well as completed work.

Large scrapbooks are used for the portfolios and work samples are organised in sections for Mathematics, English, and Integrated Topics. Each sample must be dated.

Why do we use portfolios?

At Albanvale we use portfolios to:

From "From the Classroom," *Practically Primary*, 4(1), February 1999. Reprinted with permission of the Australian Literacy Educators' Association.

- provide evidence of achievement and growth throughout a year
- provide an information-rich tool for reporting that gives parents (especially working parents who cannot get into the classroom) the opportunity to see samples of their child's work
- inform curriculum development, record keeping, and report writing
- develop an archive of the child's learning throughout their primary schooling.

The portfolios from Prep to Year 6 are retained until the children finish their primary schooling. In doing this the children's learning is mapped over an extended period. It is for these reasons that portfolios form the core of assessment and reporting processes at the school.

Who is the intended audience?

Ultimately parents and children are the main audience for the portfolios, which go home with the child towards the end of each term. Parents and children are encouraged to go through the portfolio together and in the portfolio there is a form for parents to write a short note to their child about their learning. Twice a year a formal written report is provided and at the interview parents are able to raise issues pertaining to their child's progress.

How are work samples selected for the portfolio and how is this organised?

We have certain minimum assessment tasks that are to be placed in the portfolio each year. The tasks are determined through negotiation with the teaching staff of the school. These common assessment tasks give a picture of the child's learning from Prep through to Year 6. At this stage we are still negotiating minimum requirements for Mathematics and hope to include these next year.

The minimum requirements for the portfolio are:

- a read-and-retell each semester
- a sample of the child's best handwriting each term
- a transcript from a reading and writing interview twice a year
- an integrated topic task each term
- a draft of personal writing each term
- a final copy of a piece of writing.

Work samples are mainly selected by the teacher particularly in the earlier years. This is because it is the teacher that has the greatest understanding of the curriculum goals as well as the criteria for selection of pieces. Nevertheless as children progress into the senior years of primary schooling they are able to negotiate criteria for the selection of work samples.

What can be put into a portfolio?

A diverse range of authentic assessment strategies and work samples might be included in the portfolios such as:

- samples of art work
- photographs from language experience activities
- self-published books
- teacher observations of oral language tasks
- mathematical problem solving: notes, solutions, diagrams
- self evaluation tasks
- reading journals, read-and-retells, and literature response activities
- reading, writing, spelling, and maths interviews
- pieces of work that show a process (for example, note taking, draft report, final report)
- profiles and continuums
- peer observations of cooperative group work.

A context statement must be written for every work sample in the portfolio as well as the teacher's annotation about the particular piece. The context statement is integral in providing a picture of the classroom setting, the teaching and learning leading up to the work sample being produced, and the processes that a child has moved through. Annotations are equally important in that they explicitly direct the person looking at the portfolio to growth points in the child's learning as well as providing direction for further record keeping and reporting.

The following provides some snapshots of work samples and illustrates some of the diversity and flexibility of the portfolio.

Drafts of children's writing

The following is an unconferenced extract from Sevda with the teacher's annotation:

On the holidays I went to my friend's party her name is Gulcan. A clown came to her party. He got a newspaper and put milk in it. He told us to say the magic word so we said it. It was Apadicabra. Then he terned it over to the other side but the milk did not came out. He shode us the inside but there was no milk.... (Sevda, 31 Jan 1997)

Context: This was the first writing piece collected for 1997. Children were free to choose their own topic. This is an unconferenced piece.

Content: Events written in a logical sequence. Uses time order to sequence and organise writing. Details of particular events provided.

Conventions: Most words correct or near correct.

Uses phonetic strategies and knowledge of English spelling pattern to spell unknown words, e.g., terning for turning; shode for showed.

Use of full stops, apostrophes.

Use of conjunctions.

Having written a draft, this writing was included in the portfolio and analysed. This is a very authentic way of assessing the child's work in that the context and the work sample sit right beside the growth points. In doing careful analysis of the child's writing the teacher is more able to target curriculum for the student and is able to confidently report on progress.

Showing mathematical understanding in the portfolio

The following is a written response by Adam after a unit of work on shapes. We asked the children the question, "What do you know about these shapes?" and provided pictures of several shapes as a prompt for their writing.

I know the difference between a square and a cube. Cubes are 3-D and squares are 2-D. I know the difference between a sphere and a circle. Circles are 2-D and spheres are 3-D. I know that a pentagonal prism has seven faces and five corners and five edges and a sphere has one face and no corners or edges. Pentagons, hexagons, heptagons and octagons all look a bit the same. But the difference between them is that the octagon has 8 sides the heptagon has 7 sides and a hexagon has 6 sides and the pentagon has 5 sides. All the 3-D shapes have width, length and height. (Adam, 1997)

This task gave a very clear picture of exactly what Adam knows and showed his explicit understandings of the work that had been covered. It made the task of deciding the next teaching point and the task of reporting about this aspect of mathematics very easy.

Topic based assessment

Often at the end of a topic we use concept mapping so the children can demonstrate both knowledge of the topic and also their understanding of how they link concepts together. The concept maps help inform teacher evaluation of the effectiveness of the topic.

In one assessment the children were asked to depict the main ideas they had learnt about in the topic "Plants" and were then asked to connect these in any way they thought meaningful. Their concept maps demonstrated the sense the child made about the relationships that exist within our environment. For example, Adam's concept map (see illustration) showed that he was able to link the topic "Plants" with broader understandings that were not covered in the unit. His map shows an understanding of interdependence between plants and animals. His work also shows an understanding of the basic needs of plants.

Adam's concept map

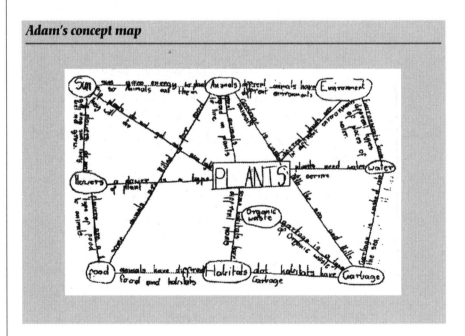

Conclusion

The portfolio is not the only assessment data gathered by teachers at Albanvale. Other data such as running records, anecdotal notes, checklists, notes about social behaviour, and judgments made on the run are other methods used to assess children. At Albanvale we believe that portfolios in conjunction with other record keeping methods are the best way in which to track the complexity and individuality of a child's learning.

> It is a philosophy that honors both the process and the products of learning as well as the active participation of the teacher and the students in their evaluation and growth. (Valencia, 1990)

REFERENCES

ACSA. (1994, June). Principles of student assessment: An ACSA policy statement. *Curriculum Perspectives, 14*(2), 38–39.

Valencia, S. (1990). A portfolio approach to classroom reading assessment: The whys, whats and hows. *The Reading Teacher, 43,* 338–340.

Making the invisible visible: The language of assessment tasks

Greer Johnson

Classroom talk about assessment tasks as problematic

The central place of talk in establishing and maintaining the teaching–learning cycle in classrooms is well documented in educational research (see Baker & Freebody, 1993, 1989; Cazden, 1988; Lemke, 1985). The problematic nature of some classroom talk in secondary and primary language classrooms has been subject to intensive scrutiny (Baker, 1997; Johnson, 1996; Freebody, Ludwig, & Gunn, 1995). An area that invites more attention is the problems associated with classroom talk about assessment tasks given to students in all curriculum areas. Although the specific assessment task discussed in this article relates to the subject English, comments made and conclusions drawn have implications across the language teaching curriculum. It is the language that constructs the tasks and the talk about the task that requires a second thought by teachers and students because it constructs certain kinds of students/subjects.

The concept of reading positions

The problematic nature of assessment tasks and the teacher's accompanying talk about the tasks can be examined through the concept of reading positions, a term generated from a critical literacy approach to the teaching of language across the curriculum. Briefly, critical literacy requires readers and writers to read between the lines of texts so as to recognise and question the ways in which the patterning of language encourages readers and writers to think and act in certain ways. This broad definition of critical literacy is elaborated on in the latter section of the article with reference to the relationship between language and power. Kress (1986) uses the term reading position:

> to indicate that any text constructs a position for its ideal reader, a kind of vantage point, a preferred point of view from which to read a text, and in

From *Literacy Learning: Secondary Thoughts*, 6(1), February 1998. Reprinted with permission of the Australian Literacy Educators' Association.

doing this indeed constructs an ideal reader. That is, texts make certain (unstated) assumptions about what their ideal readers should be, should think, should know, and should expect. The text, especially a successful text, coerces readers into that position, so that they read the text without resistance, "naturally." Of course, few readers are ideal readers, and indeed it ought to be the task of any reading [teaching] program to produce readers who are not ideal readers for any text; that is, readers who counter the text's attempts at coercion, to produce "resistant readers." (p. 209)

Curriculum materials such as the assessment task shown in Figure 1 are texts that position readers because they shape the ways in which readers are expected to respond to them. The problem is that the shaping or positioning is often invisible. Successful teaching and learning means finding ways in which assessment tasks position readers and making that positioning explicit so that students' ability to carry out the task is enhanced. Further, making visible the ways students and teachers are positioned to read and carry out assessment tasks enables informed resistance by revising the task or rewriting an alternative version. The language of assessment tasks and classroom talk across the curriculum are texts and as such should be subject to (re)evaluation at all times.

The case of unexplained shifting reading positions

Classroom context

I observed Alan teaching a lesson with a Year 11 English class in a Queensland secondary school that is situated in a low socio-economic area of a regional city. This lesson concerned a class that consisted of 20 students, male and female. The short section at the beginning of the transcribed lesson examined here is ostensibly about how students should prepare for a wide-reading test. The context of the wide-reading test is an interview between the teacher and individual students. The students have been given a set of questions and a task sheet, which includes criteria on which their work will be judged, to help them prepare to talk to the teacher about a novel they have read alone for the wide-reading program. The stated conditions are that students are to prepare for the task in their own time. Minimal teacher input is an implied condition. Alan follows the way this task is done across the subject English at his school. He did not write the task for his students. As often is the practice in school-based assessment, this task sheet was written by the Head of Department in consultation with all the teachers concerned. As such he does not have a personal investment in the literary theory/ies that underpin the task. The focus of my

Figure 1. The assessment task

YEAR 11

TASK: FICTION WIDE-READING INTERVIEW

• Perhaps the most natural way we respond to books is to talk about them—usually to friends and members of our family.

• During these exchanges we express our personal responses to issues explored, characters met, and times and places experienced in our journey with the writers.

• We (your teachers) are looking forward to discussing with you the fiction book you have read and reflected on this semester.

CONDITIONS: Preparation in student's own time

DURATION OF INTERVIEW: 10 minutes

WEIGHTING: 20%

CRITERIA: Overall effectiveness of your performance as revealed by:

CRITERIA	A	B	C	D	E
1. Selection of appropriate fiction work (sufficiently challenging and of literary merit)	☐	☐	☐	☐	☐
2. Knowledge and understanding of the main events of the novel (including setting)	☐	☐	☐	☐	☐
3. Understanding of the main issues raised in the novel	☐	☐	☐	☐	☐
4. Knowledge of major characters and understanding of the relationships they share	☐	☐	☐	☐	☐
5. Recognition and understanding of any stylistic devices used by the author	☐	☐	☐	☐	☐
6. Coherence and clarity of expression	☐	☐	☐	☐	☐
7. Appropriate vocabulary use	☐	☐	☐	☐	☐
8. Appropriateness of non–verbal features (expression, posture)	☐	☐	☐	☐	☐
9. Initiative in regard to the direction and content of the discussion	☐	☐	☐	☐	☐

analysis is the assessment task and not the teacher as individual. I am not looking for good or bad practice. The analysis shows that curriculum materials such as assessment tasks and the conditions under which they are to be performed greatly influence how English is taught and learned in any instance.

Alan introduces the lesson with:

ALAN: Good morning everyone. I will just mark the roll (*time spent marking the roll*). OK, let's make a start. Brett, hello. Can I have eyes to the front. Right, what I want to do firstly is to give you your criteria sheet for your wide-reading test, which happens next week. OK, you know that you've got to do this in your own time. You've all read your novels, I know, and you are now going through the questions that I handed out to you last week in your time (*short discussion in classroom*). Right, I'll just remind you again...waiting for your attention Colin. OK. So you know that next week will be exam week. In that exam week you'll need to come and see me and have me take your novel interview. What I would prefer you to do is to come during the time for your two doubles. Does anyone know if they have an exam that clashes with the double periods in English next week?

(*Discussion with students.*)

ALAN: OK, so what I'll have to do is this. Shh, listen please. I'll hand you a sheet at the period break. On the sheet we'll have Tuesday and Friday. On either one of those days you will put your name and it will be up to you to come to me during those periods to have your reading test done. What it will be is an oral test...what it will be is an oral test, which means that I will ask you questions about the novel and you will answer them. The main thing about this test is that you should be the person leading the test. You are in charge of the test. It's up to you to tell me what you know about the novel and to enable you to have that control of the interview. I've given you that list of questions which will enable you to have all those worked out before you come.

Reading position one: A personal response

The task statement invites the students to discuss with their teacher "the fiction book you have read and reflected on...." The social event, the teacher's "discussing with you..." attempts to mirror "the natural" way we talk to "friends and family members." This task requires the students to enact a personal transaction between the reader and the text. The focus on retelling personal response is made explicit in the second sentence of the task, which acts as a preamble to the stated criteria on the task sheet:

During these exchanges we express our personal responses to issues explored, characters met, and times and places experienced in our journey with the writers.

Subjective reading theories have been an important theoretical support to the teaching of literary texts in teacher education and in schools from the early 1980s to the present. By the 1960s liberal-humanist ideology found pedagogical space in subjective reading and writing practices (see Dixon, 1969). The literary theorists who contribute in different ways to subjective reading practices are often referred to collectively as reader-response critics. They include Rosenblatt (1969, 1978), Iser (1978), Bleich (1978), Holland (1975), and Fish (1980). The primacy of the reader's personal and literary experience is foregrounded in transacting with the text to make meaning. The author's intention has no place in this practice and the author's craft receives limited attention. Authenticity and ownership of personal "voice" issuing from personal and literary experience counts as response to reading. What some reader-response approaches would like readers to do when engaging with a literary text is illustrated by the following excerpt from a novel (Greenwald, 1980) for young adults:

> My mother thinks it all began with *Jane Eyre*, Franny Dillman wrote in her journal. She paused to remember those days—only weeks before—when she had been reading *Jane Eyre*. She's read the book by flashlight at the back of her closet....
>
> In the closet, Jane Eyre's woes were Franny's torments; Jane's passions, her passions; Jane's suffering, her very own despair. Her eyes moved from left to right, her jaw from north to south as she rhythmically chomped and reread, with fast-beating pulse and for the twentieth time, Mr. Rochester's first avowal of love for Jane Eyre. Ahhhh....
>
> How she hated the idea of Authors and Authoresses. She could hardly bring herself to look at their photographs on the backs of books. She didn't like the thought of them meddling in what she believed to be Real Life....
>
> Franny read in the closet by flashlight because reading in the closet made everything more intense. Everything but the light. Being at Thornfield Hall with Jane Eyre or at Netherfield with Elizabeth Bennett in *Pride and Prejudice* was better than anything that happened in her Daily Life. (pp. 7–11)

This short passage from the novel shows how a reader makes her own meaning by engaging in a transaction between personal feelings about characters and the text. In the space between the text and the reader, which Rosenblatt (1978) refers to as "the poem," the reader, Franny Dillman, empathises and identifies with the "passions" and "suffering" of the protagonists until they become "her very own despair." In other words, what the reader sees happening in the text is real, or at least, vicarious life. Franny gives "voice" (Gilbert, 1989) to these unique reading experiences in her journal, which is often used as a pedagogical writing companion to subjective or personalist reading strategies seen as part of "Real Life." This version of reader-response theory encourages a direct link between what is happening in the text and the reader's mind.

Within the theoretical frame of reading position one implied in the statement of the task, the characters are real people and reading is a kind of publicised personal "journey" undertaken with those characters. At this stage the response demands on the student reader are personal and ex-pressive, rather than analytical and objective. This kind of reading activity claims to develop readers whose unique life experiences are validated through the literature they read and write. Reader-response literary theory encourages a sharing of individual values and beliefs between the reader and the text. A pedagogical maxim is that all personal responses are val-ued equally. The valuing of the personal response is called into question when the requirements of the task statement shifts to a different reading po-sition in the accompanying statement of criteria one to five by which stu-dents' responses to the novel will be judged. Austin (1996) argues that:

> Becoming a (competent) student-of-literature means being able to adapt to the requirements of particular ways of reading even if those ways are not themselves talked about explicitly. (p. 135)

By extension, this analysis raises questions about the kinds of reading practice shifts that students are expected to make in assessment tasks in the subject English as well as in other curriculum areas without explicit in-struction about how to negotiate those shifts.

Reading position two: A text and author analysis

The shift of reading positions becomes visible by taking a closer look at criteria one to five from the same critical literacy view of language expressed earlier, and a different literary theory perspective. As criteria six to nine deal with the presentation of the response to the novel in the interview con-text, they are not addressed in this article. In the first five criteria the students are asked to analyse literary devices portraying events, issues, characters, and stylistic devices used by the author of an appropriately challenging and meritorious work of fiction. There is the assumption that there is now an objective, unified reading of the various novels that all student readers can find in the text. The required reading practices have changed. The ideal student reader is expected to think and speak differently about the novel. Instead of expressing "personal responses," as stated in the task, readers are now being asked in the criteria to deliver a mix of text- and author-focused critical analysis to fiction. Although the reader is positioned by the wording of criteria one to five to adopt the role of master critic and to seek literary truths through close textual analysis of "quality" texts there are further adjustments to be made within this reading position. Reading position two, version one, is represented in criteria one to four, which are supported by new critical theory that is practised as close reading of the text as an artistic object in itself: a verbal icon (see Wimsatt & Beardsley, 1954). Meaning is to be found within the language and structure of the words on the page. The terms "selection of appropriate fiction work (sufficiently challenging and of literary merit)" places criterion one within the frame of new criticism, which values universal readings derived from canonical fiction. Continued use of terms such as "the main events," "the main issues," and "major characters" also confirms the task's requirement for a universal reading.

In criterion five the mention of the author in relation to stylistic devices demands an adjusted form of objective analysis from the reader: reading position two, version two. The "recognition and understanding of any stylistic devices used by the author" is framed by the reading practice of interpreting "authorial intentionality." Wimsatt and Beardsley (1954), arguing from a text-focused new critical frame, call this practice "intentional fallacy," which challenges the notion that a reader can successfully second guess the meaning inside the author's head. The objective reader is further positioned by criteria five to arrive at a universal interpretation through close reading of the words on the page as well as of the author's intentions in choosing particular words/stylistic devices. Again personal response is not invoked. The conversational tone necessary for a "natural talk" required in the task statement has shifted to "procedural displays" (Bloome, 1985) in criteria one to five.

No space for a critique of reading positions one and two

The wide-reading task outlined in Figure 1 is positioning readers to take up two major shifting reading positions and practices: subjective response (in the task statement) and objective critical analysis—versions one and two (in the criteria). In the introduction to the lesson, Alan mentions the criteria but not the negative implications for misreading the positioning. The problematic nature of the classroom about the assessment involves the shifting practices of reading as well as the fact that the shifts remain invisible to the student-reader during this lesson. The reading positions are not made available to the students because of the specified conditions of the task: preparation in the student's own time. The following extract from the lesson shows that at least one student wants to go on discussing the reading test.

ALAN: In either of the doubles. Everyone has to do it in either of those two days. Tuesday periods one and two, Friday periods five and six. Right. So next week just make sure you know. OK. Periods one and two and that's Tuesday, and periods five and six and that's Friday, you are coming to see me for your...reading test. Write it in your diaries now please. Write it in your diaries (*the students write*). Right, the week after this will happen...Tuesday periods one and two. Stimulus Writing Task. OK. Note it down. (*Late arrival of student.*) I'm just going through with everyone what your examinations will take up for the next couple of weeks. You've got the reading tests coming up next week. You need to come and see me either period one or two next Tuesday or periods five and six next Friday and you will need to write down a time to come to see me—for that I will give you a piece of paper. In the final week you'll have the stimulus task. Now for this task here next week you will spend this Friday afternoon working on this task so you will have this Friday afternoon to get organised for your reading test. So what do you think we're doing today, Angus? What about this? The way we are going to look at the stimulus task. How to do a stimulus writing task?

STUDENT: Couldn't we do the reading test first?

ALAN: No....

In not discussing and interrogating the "reading test," no account of the task is made available for scrutiny. An opportunity to monitor the curriculum by evaluating and critiquing curriculum materials such as the assessment task is lost for teacher and students. The request for further talk about the test may indicate that the student sees a problem. Observational data suggests that the student wanted to spend more time discussing the task. The condition of the task (preparation in student's own time) has blocked the student's request to continue the talk about the assessment task, subverted the student's agenda, and compounded the power of classroom contexts to position students implicitly as particular kinds of readers in English. Extended talk between teacher and students about reading practices and supporting literary theories might counterbalance that positioning because it might lead to an understanding of invisibly fragmentary reading (and speaking) positions required for successful performance of the task. Talk between teachers and students might also lead to the formulation of practical ways in which the two main reading positions might become mutually supportive. For example, how language strategies and stylistic devices portraying events, issues, and characters help produce personal and text-focused responses and interpretations. Such an understanding might lead also to a discussion of the kinds of reading positions that are excluded from this assessment task. For example, a critical literacy interpretation of texts based on a group of literary theories that are generally known as post-structuralist (see Mellor & Patterson, 1996). From this theoretical perspective interpretations or readings are generated on the basis that texts are constructed in ways that are shaped by and shape particular views of the world. Readers make meaning of texts according to their social experiences, values, historicity, and ideological or cultural views of the world. Recognition of the relationship between language and power is a key concept. The link between language and power made within a critical literacy approach to the teaching of language is called on in the final section of this article as a means of re-evaluating this instance of classroom talk about the assessment task. I now reread a section of the classroom talk for the ways in which it constructs social practices of power in the classroom.

Assuring the favour of the dominated

Ironically, in the extract of the lesson repeated below, Alan is telling his students that they have control of the reading test.

ALAN: What it will be will be an oral test...which means that I will ask you questions about the novel and you will answer them. The main thing about this test is that you should be the person leading the test. You are in charge of the test. It's up to you to tell me what you know about the novel and to enable you to have that control of the interview. I've given you that list of questions, which will enable you to have all those worked out before you come.

Paoletti (1990: 195) likens this kind of "empowerment" of students in the classroom to Machiavelli's approach to war (Machiavelli, 1513/1974, 44), which she translates from Italian as:

always, although one may be very strong in armed forces, yet in entering the province one needs to assure the favour of the dominated.

The students' power to choose the times to lead the test masks the power of the language of the task to dictate the reading and speaking positions that the students must adopt if they are to be judged as successful readers of their novel. As argued above, the power over what counts as good reading resides in at least two shifting reading positions embedded and entangled in the statement of the task and its accompanying criteria. The students are hardly "in charge of the test" at all. The classroom talk around the task merely serves "to assure the favour of the dominated." Being in charge of the test—preparing it without explicit teaching of the considerable demands—is potentially disempowering.

Whose English is this?

Delpit (1992) argues that explicit teaching really can make a difference because it can bridge the gap between culturally exclusive and culturally inclusive discourses of reading and writing. Concerns about whether or not teachers and students appreciate the shifts necessary to become competent readers (of both novels and assessment tasks) are linked to important political considerations. Further, below the surface of this seemingly friendly task are important socio-cultural queries. They are not related solely to the mix of reading positions but rather to the culturally exclusive nature of both reading positions offered to students. The political question that English teachers must ask is, for whom is this task not natural? The assumption that students discuss their personal responses to fiction with friends and other members of their family might be accurate for some students, but few schools can make this assumption. Additionally, personal response teaches a kind of literacy that is in danger of locking students into an uncritical way of looking at what they read and their reading practices. In other words, the "issues explored" may be recognised as personally relevant but their cultural and social origin will most probably not be questioned. By looking to criteria one to five, non-mainstream readers will be marginalised further. Two examples support this point: firstly, the designation of "appropriate fiction work (sufficiently challenging and of literary merit)" is not consistent across cultural contexts; and, secondly, the examination of "main issues raised in the novel" is also a culturally specific criterion and is therefore disempowering for some readers if they are not offered opportunities for an interrogation of those issues.

Conclusions

This article has reflected upon a wide-reading assessment task presented to students during a lesson in the subject English. The discussion highlights the problems for student readers who in this instance are expected to negotiate the rocky terrain across subjective and objective reading positions and even make further shifts within the objective reading position. The paucity of classroom talk about the shifting reading positions is explained in terms of the (limiting) conditions of the task that specify that students will prepare for the task in their own time. The point of examining the wording of assessment task sheet and criteria, as well as the classroom talk from a critical literacy perspective, is to show how these texts are not neutral and that their language represents and shapes relations of power for students and teachers. They must be examined for compatibility of the literary theory/ies that support them in addition to being situated in particular classroom contexts and sets of conditions. A key point being made in this article is not that the wide-reading task is impossible for students to carry out successfully or that the teacher performed badly. Rather, it has been argued that knowledge acquired through classroom talk based on a systematic analysis of the required reading positions and the specified conditions for engaging with the text might make the teaching-learning-assessment cycle less problematic for all concerned. What counts as reading in this instance in the subject English is an invisibly fragmented practice, and the conditions of the task do not enable the teacher to render the invisible visible.

Looking beyond the subject English, in the busy world of teaching how often are assessment tasks revised through amalgamation with little time for attention to the theory and practice nexus? How often in school-based assessment are students given an assessment task and asked to prepare it in their own time with minimal teacher input? How often in non-school-based assessment is the language of assessment tasks beyond the control of the teacher? The analysis in this article suggests two ways of ensuring an equitable teaching and learning outcome. Firstly, it is important for writers of assessment tasks to consider the theoretical implications of assessment tasks and the human and material resources that are available to students in completing the required task. Secondly, across all subjects a primary consideration for teachers is the teaching of language in use. Although the teaching of critical literacy is becoming a recognised method for studying curriculum texts in a critically reflective manner, the logical extension is the application of critical literacy to texts such as assessment tasks and classroom talk in a move to make the invisible visible.

REFERENCES

Austin, H. (1996). Reading positions and the student-of-literature in a Year 6 classroom. *Australian Journal of Language and Literacy, 19*(2), 135–144.

Baker, C.D. (1997). Literacy practices and classroom order. In S. Muspratt, A. Luke, & P. Freebody (Eds.), *Constructing critical literacies: Teaching and learning textual practices* (pp. 243–261). Creskill NJ: Hampton Press.

Baker, C.D., & Freebody, P. (1989). Talk around text: Constructions of textual and teacher authority in classroom discourse. In S.D. Castell, A. Luke, & C. Luke (Eds.), *Language, authority and criticism readings on the school textbook* (pp. 263–283). London: Falmer.

Baker, C.D., & Freebody, P. (1993). The crediting of literate competence in classroom talk. *Australian Journal of Language and Literacy, 16*(4), 279–294.

Bleich, D. (1978). *Subjective criticism*. Baltimore, MD: Johns Hopkins University Press.

Bloome, D. (1985). Reading as a social process. *Language Arts, 62*(2), 134–142.

Cazden, C. (1988). *Classroom discourse: The language of teaching and learning*. Portsmouth, NH: Heinemann.

Delpit, L. (1992). Acquisition of the literate discourse: Bowing before the master? *Theory Into Practice, 21*(4), 296–302.

Dixon, J. (1969). *Growth through English* (2nd ed.). London: Oxford University Press.

Fish, S.E. (1980). *Is there a text in this class? The authority of interpretative communities*. Cambridge, MA: Harvard University Press.

Freebody, P., Ludwig, C., & Gunn, S. (1995). *Everyday literacy practice in and out of school in low socio-economic urban communities*. Centre for Literacy Education Research, Griffith University.

Gee, J.P. (1990). *Social linguistics and literacies: Ideology in discourses*. London: Falmer.

Gilbert, P. (1989). *Writing, schooling, and deconstruction: From voice to text in the classroom*. London: Routledge and Kegan Paul.

Greenwald, S. (1980). *It all began with Jane Eyre: Or the secret life of Franny Dillman*. Harmondsworth: Puffin Plus.

Holland, N. (1975). *Five readers reading*. New Haven, CT: Yale University Press.

Iser, W. (1978). *The act of reading: A theory of aesthetic response*. London: Routledge & Kegan Paul.

Johnson, G. (1996). *Teaching English as a non-unitary S/subject: A post-personalist account of practice*. Unpublished doctoral thesis, University of Queensland, Australia.

Kress, G. (1985). *Linguistic processes in sociocultural practice*. Geelong: Deakin University Press.

Kress, G. (1986). Interrelations of reading and writing. In A. Wilkinson (Ed.), *The writing of writing* (pp. 198–214). Philadelphia: Milton Keynes.

Kress, G. (1988). Language as a social practice. In G. Kress (Ed.), *Communication and culture: An introduction* (pp. 78–129). Kensington: New South Wales University Press.

Lemke, J. (1985). *Using language in the classroom*. Deakin: Deakin University Press.

Machiavelli, N. (1513/1974). *Il Principe (The Prince)*. Fierenze, Italy: Sansoni.

Mellor, B. & Patterson, A. (1996). *Investigating texts*. Collesloe, WA: Chalkface Press.

Paoletti, I. (1990). *Social structure as collective imagery: Three studies in educational settings*. Unpublished doctoral thesis, University of New England, Australia.

Making the invisible visible:
The language of assessment tasks
101

Rosenblatt, L. (1969). Towards a transactional theory of reading. *Journal of Reading Behaviour, 1*(1), 31–47.

Rosenblatt, L. (1978). *The reader, the text, the poem: The transactional theory of the literary work.* Carbondale, IL: Southern Illinois University Press.

Wimsatt, W.K., & Beardsley, M.C. (1954). *The verbal icon: Studies in the meaning of poetry.* Lexington, KY: University of Kentucky Press.

Reading assessment options for teachers of junior secondary students

Michael McNamara

The purpose of this paper is to consider a range of alternatives for teachers wishing to assess students' reading abilities and behaviours in the junior secondary school and comment on their usefulness. It will be argued that teachers should be aware of the strengths and weaknesses of all options, that those options which seem to offer most stimulating information about students' performance are difficult to implement, and that compromise between what is best and what is possible is a likely component of choosing between means of assessment.

What is the purpose of the assessment?

In a discussion of the purposes of assessment, Broadfoot (1987) specified the difference between assessment for curriculum, assessment for communication, and assessment for accountability. Assessment for curriculum is that which is diagnostic and motivating. It tells the teacher what each pupil has learned, more general information about students' strengths and weaknesses, and how far the teaching has succeeded in its aims. Assessment for communication has a certification function and a selection function. Assessment for accountability is to demonstrate the extent to which the aims of an educational institution have been fulfilled. Broadfoot also reminds us of the distinction between formative and summative assessment, defining the former as a means to encourage learning, and suggesting that the emphasis of the latter is to provide reliable and acceptable information on what has been achieved.

As discussed below, secondary teachers should be clear on the general purposes of assessment and be sure to choose means of assessing students which meet their specific needs.

Assessment for curriculum: Diagnostic and motivating

An assessment mechanism which involves the teacher and student in collaboration, and includes close scrutiny of the process of reading, examination of

From *The Australian Journal of Language and Literacy*, 15(4), November 1992. Reprinted with permission of the Australian Literacy Educators' Association.

the text which is read, and consideration of the context of reading, is likely to stimulate detailed diagnosis and motivate teachers and students to take immediate and appropriate action to continue reading development.

There are a number of reasons for choosing a means of assessment with these characteristics. Law (1984) calls for collaboration between teachers and students in the assessment process. He argues that this acknowledges students' responsibility for the way in which they are portrayed. Close scrutiny of the process of reading gives teachers the opportunity to design activities that are appropriate for each student. Examination of the text that is being read involves the teacher in reflection about the demands of the text and the kinds of support that learning readers will need in handling that text and others like it. Consideration of the context of reading gives the teacher the opportunity to reflect on the environmental and other factors that could affect reading behaviour. The influence of this sort of factor is acknowledged in standardised tests. In the *TORCH Manual* (Mossenson et al., 1987, p. 7), teachers are advised to administer the test in the morning and in a suitable room.

Assessment for curriculum using close observation

In the following section, a recording of one Year 8 student reading and discussing a passage required in a Social Education class, is analysed. The act of reading/doing the analysis makes clear the sort of support the student requires to make sense of the passage and others like it. The analysis is intended to demonstrate the potential richness of close observation.

The student, S, discusses the passage reproduced below. It should be noted that S read the passage aloud quite fluently and the retelling was done after she had time to re-read the passage silently. The passage itself was part of a longer document used in the fourth term of the previous year in S's Year 7 class.

Ancient Egypt: Pyramids and Herodotus

Almost two and a half thousand years ago Herodotus, an ancient Greek historian, visited the land of the Egyptians. He travelled into the desert to see the great pyramid at Giza. In the history he wrote later, Herodotus described the largest pyramid of the Pharaoh Khufu or Cheops.

It took twenty years to build and has a square base and its height is equal to the length on each side. It is made of polished stone blocks and all of them at least nine metres long and beautifully fitted together.

When Herodotus saw the pyramid they were already two thousand years old and the Egyptians themselves had forgotten many of the facts about the construction and how their ancestors had come to build these immense tombs.

S: "This was about...two and a half thousand years ago and it is about an ancient Greek historian named Herodotus and he went to Egypt and he had um built the pyramids and when he came...like he hadn't seen them for about 2000 or something years ago, he didn't see them, and all the Egyptians forgot how to make the pyramids and that and they were very big and they were made out of shiny tomby stones and that is about it."

Table 1 lists the points made in the passage. The points that are marked with an asterisk in the right hand column are those that the student was able to repeat in her first retelling.

Table 1

Herodotus was an ancient Greek historian.	*
2,500 years ago, Herodotus visited Egypt.	*
He traveled to the desert to visit the pyramid at Giza.	
The pyramids were two thousand years old when he saw them.	*
Details of how the pyramids were built were not known by the Egyptians living in Herodotus's time.	
Herodotus wrote the following about the pyramid:	
It took twenty years to build.	
It had a square base.	*
Its height is equal to the length of each side.	
It is made of polished stone blocks.	*
All of the stones are least nine metres long.	
The stones beautifully fitted together.	

In this retelling it appears as if S was able to repeat some significant information but her understanding seems largely confused about time, who had in fact built the pyramids, and Herodotus's role.

The text itself is noteworthy in the following ways:

- The passage is from a unit about Ancient Egypt but starts with a description of an Ancient Greek historian.
- The passage includes a quote from Herodotus's writing. It requires that the reader be familiar with the convention of marking a substantial quotation with an indentation.
- While the concept of time is central to the passage, the time segments are not ordered sequentially.

The passage refers to three segments of time, they are:

  A   The time of the building of the pyramids;

B A time in Egypt two thousand years later when a Greek visitor came to Egypt;

C The time of Herodotus writing the history of the pyramid's construction.

The three segments occur in the passage in the following order: B, C, A, B, A. In the sweep of three paragraphs, four and a half thousand years are covered but they are referred to in two easily confused two thousand year blocks.

The assessor and S discussed the passage further.

A OK. There is one thing that just when you were telling me about it, I wasn't clear on. You said that he went to visit Egypt and then you said something about the pyramids. Could you just say that again. What was he doing there?

S I think he was building he was writing on how they were building a pyramid.

A All right. Were they building them at the time he visited?

S Yeah.

A Do you want to check that?

S While he was visiting there it took twenty years to build so he was there and umm.... No when he saw them they were two thousand years old.

A All right. So what are....

S He wasn't actually there. When he came back...when he saw they were two thousand years old, the pyramids.

A So how do you mean when he came back? Had he been there before?

S Yeah

A Just take your time. You are a really terrific reader, S. Don't let me panic you.

S Yeah, it says here he travelled to see the great pyramid at Giza, right, and in the history he wrote later a book on it and when, yeah...and he described the largest pyramid and now he says how long it took to build the pyramid and it says here when Herodotus saw the pyramid they were two thousand years ago.

In the last attempt at a retelling the student seems surer. She has a much greater sense of the way time is organised in the passage; she is surer that Herodotus's writing has been quoted although there is a sense that she is still not totally at ease with the passage.

What does this brief analysis suggest about assessment? At the beginning of this section it was suggested that "assessment for curriculum" would involve close scrutiny of the process of reading, examination of the text which is read, consideration of the context of reading, and teacher and student acting in collaboration.

Close scrutiny of the process of reading

The analysis shows that S is a very competent decoder of the material she is expected to use in class; that she can struggle to express her understanding when put under pressure; but when encouraged, she can make some sense of quite challenging material.

Examination of the text which is read

The analysis suggests that teachers who use factual material similar to that described above might read it carefully before presenting it in class to see the kinds of difficulty it presents. Teachers could reflect on the background knowledge the students would need to have before they could make best use of the passage. The teachers might note the difficulties presented when moments of history are written about out of sequence.

Consideration of the context of reading

S read and summarised the passage in a one to one conference with a researcher who was not a teacher at the school in a room adjacent to the classroom. One cannot be sure simply from the retelling how her reading was affected by it occurring in these circumstances. Nevertheless, it is clear that when S was given time and encouragement to clarify her summary, she was able to come to a closer understanding of the text by re-reading it and continuing to describe what she understood. Teachers might reflect on the possibility of giving students the opportunity to articulate their understanding to a sympathetic audience (perhaps the student's peers in small group activities). They might also reflect on whether the dynamics of their classrooms are conducive to creating audiences for reading so that understanding can be developed by summariser and listener together.

Teacher and student in collaboration

The process described above brings the teacher and student face to face in a shared experience that can become a stimulus for further growth and a reference point for shared analysis and discussion.

As well, it is clear that the teacher intervenes in the reading assessment process so that half-formed understandings are explored and developed. Other writers have called for this type of intervention. Brozo (1990) advocates what he calls "interactive assessment," the goal of which "is to discover the conditions under which a student will succeed in reading rather than merely describing a student's current status as a reader." Kletzien and Bednar (1990) describe "dynamic assessment" which attempts not only to recognise already mastered abilities but also to identify capabilities that "are in the process of maturing."

The question arises about when and where such detailed attention to the performance of a single student can occur. The student whose reading and discussion are described above participated in a one to one interview lasting fifteen to twenty minutes. To conduct this sort of interview for each of the students in a single class, let alone all the classes a teacher might have, would take a prohibitively long time. An alternative is for teachers to set class time aside in which they observe students at work and then keep an informal record of their observations. This requires a sufficiently orderly class for this sort of observation to be possible and the ability of students in the class to work without disturbing the teacher and student in conference. If these conditions are satisfied, then the assessment process that involves close scrutiny of a student's reading not only provides evidence upon which to base written assessment, it stimulates thought about classroom reading material and ways to assist students to read effectively.

Assessment for curriculum and standardised tests

A criticism levelled at standardised tests is that the use of them denies the teacher the opportunity of observing how a reader makes meaning of a particular text, instead restricting the teacher to being a receiver of a report of reading ability (Johnston, 1989). The teacher, for example, cannot be sure whether students have re-read a piece before committing themselves to paper, or revised their position after an initial attempt. Standardised tests cannot describe the inexact, or half-formed understanding that students can have about a passage, the sort of understanding that is developed and clarified with another's prompts and suggestions. This sort of description is possible when teachers closely observe and interact with students during the assessment process.

A further problem with standardised tests is that there is little opportunity for teachers to consider the demands of the material being read, its similarity to the material that they will require students to use in their subjects, or the way that the purpose of reading (for assessment, for enjoyment, for performance, for information gathering) can affect the way that it is read. A fundamental principle of standardised tests is that we should conceptualise reading as a skill or set of skills which can be articulated in relation to students independent of the particular texts that they are reading. It may be the case, though, that a key item of vocabulary or unfamiliar schematic structure (as in the case described above) could affect the students' understanding or result in relation to a certain skill, while a different result might occur if the tested passage is something different. Standardised test results cannot offer insights into students' performance on reading in content area subjects, because there are not tests which can take into account the breadth of subject areas or the diversity of styles that are possible in content area reading. Understanding of the demands of reading in various situations can best be gauged by observing the reading that occurs in them.

There are standardised tests which do claim to be diagnostic and able to suggest appropriate courses of future action for teachers. The writers of the *Tests of Reading Comprehension (TORCH) Manual* claim that theirs are tests able to be interpreted with reference to particular skills. They give examples of the kind of skills that might become the focus of attention with particular students:

> Susan has a TORCH score of 32 which suggests that she can complete rephrased sentences as well as connect pronouns with previously mentioned nouns. She may not be able to connect ideas separated in text as well as extracting details in the presence of distracting ideas. (Mossenson et al., 1987, p. 17)

The writers suggest that this is one of the features that makes TORCH a useful package. Nevertheless, one fears that emphasis on such skills might prompt teachers to develop them by encouraging students to read and complete activities identical to the activities required in the test. "Teaching to the test" is lamented in a variety of literature (e.g., Cambourne & Turbill, 1991; Johnston, 1989). Mastery of such skills is still no guarantee of mastery of the diversity of reading likely to be encountered at school.

Assessment for communication: Certification and selection

Broadfoot (1987) reminds us of other purposes of assessment, namely certification and selection. When assessment serves the selection function it is necessarily comparative and often competitive. There are a number of possibilities for certification and selection. Assessment can be descriptive, norm-referenced, criterion-referenced, or work-referenced.

Garforth and Macintosh (1986) give examples of descriptive assessment where student performance is recorded in terms of tasks required, goals set, and the skills demonstrated by the student once the task is completed. Descriptive assessment can also document change in students' performance. It can describe typical behaviour before the teaching/learning sequence begins and changes that have occurred during the course. The reference point is the individual child's starting behaviour. There need be no requirement that the tasks be uniform, so direct comparison may be difficult. When this is the case, interpretation is left to the reader who assumes responsibility for attaching weight to various aspects of the description. With regard to reading, interpretation depends on the reader's understanding of the process of reading, the various skills and knowledge required to make reading material meaningful, and his/her familiarity with the material actually read by the student.

Criterion-referenced assessment is a potential way of making the process of interpreting assessment less demanding. In relation to reading, if the criteria for assessment are intended to describe a full range of reading ability, then placing a student in relation to the criteria makes explicit the assessor's opinion about what has been achieved and what has yet to be achieved. Placing a student's reading behaviour by describing it in terms of predetermined criteria relieves the reader of the assessment of the responsibility of deciding the extent of the student's achievement. Similarly, if the criteria are defined hierarchically in a way that does not offend the reader of the assessment, then comparison between students becomes easier and selection simpler. As is indicated above, results of TORCH tests can be given in terms of predetermined and hierarchically defined criteria. Another example in Victoria is the use of criteria by which Victorian Certificate of Education Common Assessment Tasks are graded.

Work-referenced assessment indicates completion of a specified number of work requirements. Certificates record the assessment simply in terms of S or N. The student either has or has not completed the specified minimum number of work requirements. In this form of assessment, performance is not graded.

Norm-referencing is another way of distinguishing between students for selection. Norm-referencing occurs after the test activity and is designed to place a student's performance in relation to others' performance. It does not describe reading behaviour in itself. (As is pointed out by Griffin and Nix [1991, pp. 88–89], informal norm-referencing can take the form of assessment for curriculum. They argue that every time a teacher judges what it is reasonable to expect from a particular student, the implicit standards for assessment are the teacher's own judgements about the capabilities of a wider group of students displaying similar characteristics. This might be limiting or enriching depending on the teacher's expectations and previous experiences.)

Assessment for accountability

Broadfoot suggests that "an educational institution must increasingly be able to demonstrate to both itself and the world outside that it is fulfilling the aims that it has set for itself and the ones expected of it by society in general" (1987, p. 5), and that this has implications for assessment. Some argue that this requirement results in the demand for a readily-defined, comprehensive set of criteria defined publicly before the assessment tasks are completed. This point is made in the introduction to the Victorian Ministry of Education and Training's *English Profiles Handbook*.

> Assessment of a more formal and systematic kind is necessary to ensure that students are making progress in all aspects of a subject. Formal assessments include planned assessment tasks designed to provide information about students' work in relation to specific criteria. (1991, p. 7)

Assessment of reading behaviour for accountability at the system level, it is argued, must be comprehensive, but structured with sufficient simplicity to make comparison over time possible.

One senses, again, that such constraints must inevitably involve compromise. The analysis of the student reading the passage about Herodotus and the pyramids above, gives the beginning of an insight into the complexity of the reading process, how successful reading depends not only on the use of skills that can be brought to every reading situation but on the interaction between reader and text, the student's prior knowledge of the subject of the reading, the vocabulary specific to it, and the attitude the reader brings to the process of reading. Such detail may become too burdensome if the purpose of assessment is for accountability. One (perhaps compromised) solution to this problem that appears to have been implemented up until the present is to describe reading behaviour in terms of *skills and activities without reference to context or material being read*. There is an elaboration of this point in the section below.

How comprehensive is the assessment?

The most detailed methods of assessment are those which enable description of reading behaviour, the texts being read, and the contexts of reading—that is, the environment the reading is done in, the purpose of the reading, the audience for the reading, and the expectations that the audience has of the reader. In this paper, it has been argued that the more detailed the assessment, the greater chance of more useful diagnostic feedback for the teacher. However, detailed assessment is not a guarantee of comprehensive assessment. In the detailed example given above, although there was a lot of useful description of S's reading of the passage about Herodotus, one might be reluctant to generalise on the basis of that reading about S's ability to read other texts.

This is a problem for all kinds of assessment. It has been addressed by distinguishing the concept of "generalisable" reading skills from the concept of particular reading skills-in-use. Practically, there is a risk with individualised assessment of skill-in-use that particular passages which are being read while the student is observed may not give the reader the opportunity to demonstrate all the abilities that he or she has. This problem has been dealt with by predetermining a comprehensive set of skills which become criteria for assessment and which can guide observation of student reading behaviour. Necessarily, these are limited constructs. This can be seen by comparison of two descriptions of sets of desirable skills. They are those used to describe levels of achievement in the *Test of Reading Comprehension (TORCH) Manual* and the *English Profiles Handbook*. It should be noted that the levels of achievement taken from the latter are very brief summaries of behaviours and abilities that are described in much greater detail in various reading bands groupings of descriptors which teachers can match to the performance of their students. Nevertheless the comparison is instructive.

The English Profiles and the Test of Reading Comprehension are designed for different bodies of students, the Profiles being relevant from P–12, while TORCH is intended for use with Years 3 to 10. Nevertheless, there are clear differences between the ways students' potential performances are described. The English Profiles include behaviours ("talks confidently about characters") and attitudes ("likes to look at books and have stories read") in relation to a range of text types as well as skills of comprehension and analysis. The other describes performance in many instances in terms of behaviour required by the test itself ("connects pronouns with previously mentioned nouns"). The comparison must make one suspicious of the degree of comprehensiveness that scales like those above can claim. Recognising this, the designers of the Reading Profiles add sections for the teacher to note behaviours, attitudes, and skills not accounted for in the descriptors and provide space for teachers to note the type of material being read and the context in which it is read. Such flexibility was not available to the TORCH designers. Indeed, full use of the Profiles requires close observation similar to that described in the section above.

Table 2

TORCH	ENGLISH PROFILES
Infer emotion from a few scattered clues and the writer's tone	Is skilful in analysing and inter-preting wide range of written material.
Reconstruct the writer's general message from specific statements	Has clear ideas about purposes for reading. Reads beyond the literal in search of deeper meaning.
Provide evidence of having understood a motive underlying a series of actions	Reads widely for learning and pleasure and can readily draw together main ideas. Has a critical and analytical outlook towards ideas and writing style.
Provide a detail in the presence of competing answers	Can read different kinds of texts. Interprets and analyses passages and explains personal responses.
Provide a detail in the presence of distracting ideas	Knows how to tackle difficult texts. Experiences with reading reflected in own writing and general knowledge. Talks confidently about characters and settings in literature.
Connect ideas separated in text	Expects what is read to make sense. Talks about what is read and indicates understanding. Absorbs language and ideas.
Connect pronouns with previously mentioned nouns	Seeks meaning from printed text. Wants to read a lot and talk about stories.
Complete rephrased sentences	Is able to recognise many familiar words and tries to read unfamiliar text. Shows signs of becoming an active reader.
Complete very simple rewordings	Knows how a book works, likes to look at books and have stories read.
Complete sentences copied verbatim	
Provide subject of story given multiple references	

What are the reference points or criteria for the assessment?

The discussion above has already touched on this question. It is worth re-capping.

The assessor's reading

When student S was observed reading the passage about Herodotus in Ancient Egypt, the teacher based his assessment of S's performance on his own interpretation of the passage. This involved him in examination of the passage and as a result the prerequisites for reading it successfully became clear.

The student's prior reading behaviour

In future assessment of S's reading behaviour, aspects of her performance detailed above will help determine criteria for growth. Will she be more confident to read over passages that seem immediately inaccessible? Will she acknowledge her doubts about her own understanding—a part of the continuum between self-monitoring and self-correcting? Will she demonstrate behaviour of a reader who is used to being in control of a wide variety of reading material? If she does these things, she will have made significant steps forward. But those criteria will not describe the full range of S's reading ability or behaviour.

Preordinate criteria

Predetermined, or preordinate, criteria offer the security of a reference point from which to make judgements about a broad range of reading abilities. They offer the chance to make comparison between students across schools and over time. However, as has been shown, they are not exhaustive and they might not be sufficiently discriminating to measure significant growth in individual students including their growth shown in particular subjects.

How valid is the assessment?

Much of the discussion of methods of assessment is conducted in terms of their validity, that is the quality of being well-founded and applicable to the students and the circumstances in question. Thus, the writers of the *English Profiles Handbook* argue "entire dependence on informal methods of assessment can mean that coverage of important skills and knowledge may be incomplete for some students, thus limiting their success" (Ministry of Education and Training, Victoria, 1991, p. 7).

On the other hand, there is very vocal condemnation of standardised tests. Kemp (1989) doubts the suitability of tests to monitor the performance of struggling readers. He suggests that the very act of conducting a formal test (in rows, in silence) can be intimidating enough to deny students the chance of displaying their best talents. Tuinman (1986) argues in *Reading is Recognition When Reading is Not Reasoning* that reading comprehension tests assess only formal comprehension which he differentiates from communicative comprehension and private comprehension. Formal comprehension, he argues, is the most complex, involving the ability to utilize a range of skills: the reader has to understand details, relate them to other information presented, make fine distinctions among facts, events, and motives, and recognise and understand abstractions. He suggests that this sort of comprehension involves reasoning, which is not a characteristic of all reading, and adds that, one of the most curious developments in measurements of reading comprehension is that concepts and techniques suitable for the measurement of formal comprehension have come to be used for the measurement of all comprehension! Brown and Cambourne (1989) are quite adamant, "Language is an ever changing medium that always presents new challenges even as we learn to control more. It is qualitative and subjective and therefore must be approached differently when evaluation is considered. Evaluation by testing is not applicable to language."

What view of reading underpins the assessment?

It is impossible to ascribe a view of reading to the designers and users of particular assessment techniques because the measurement devices themselves are not such flexible things that they can be made to reflect every aspect of the designer's understanding. Compromises may have to be made in the design and use of any means of assessment. Assessment of reading ability must be conceptualised in terms of practicality and utility as well as in terms of reading theory.

Nevertheless, close scrutiny of the process of reading over time allows for observation of reading behaviour in relation to a range of texts and in a number of contexts. Such a process is consistent with a view of reading which suggests that reading skill is inseparable from reading material and that skill is only possessed or shown in the act of reading. Use of standardised tests and scales of reading behaviour is consistent with a view that reading can be divided into a hierarchy of isolatable and generalisable skills.

What means of assessment should be used?

As has been suggested, the issue of assessment is a complex one. Choice of means of assessment involves consideration of the needs of the teachers and students involved, the intended audience of the assessment, and the amount of time available for assessment.

You might consider these questions:

Is the assessment for diagnostic purposes?

Will the assessment give you the "opportunity to assess the instructional factors that influence reading performance" (Brozo, 1990)?

Is the assessment going to be the basis for formal reporting?

What skills will the reader or hearer of the assessment be able to bring to the reading or the interview so that description can be interpreted meaningfully?

To what extent is the assessment linked to certification? Is any link with certification appropriate?

Do you have a role in making assessments which show the extent to which the school is fulfilling its aims?

How influenced in the junior level are you by requirements for certification and selection that mark formal assessment at the senior level?

If you imitate practices at the senior level, how flexible are they? Are they useful for the full range of your students?

It will probably be the case that choice of assessment mechanisms will involve compromise. When teachers are aware of the compromises, and why various types of assessment have been developed, they will be in a better position to make what will always be a difficult decision.

REFERENCES

Broadfoot, P. (1987). *Introducing profiling: A practical manual*. London: Macmillan Education.

Brown, H., & Cambourne, B. (1989). Evaluation in the whole language classroom: A collaborative research project. In E. Daly (Ed.), *Monitoring children's language development*. Melbourne: Australian Reading Association.

Brozo, W.G. (1990). Learning how at-risk readers learn best: A case for interactive assessment. *Journal of Reading, 33*, 522–527.

Cambourne, B., & Turbill, J. (1991). Evaluation and the literacy curriculum: Who is in control? *Australian Journal of Reading, 14*(3).

Garforth, D., & Macintosh, H. (1986). *Profiling: A user's manual*. Cheltenham, UK: Stanley Thornes Limited.

Griffin, P., & Nix, P. (1991). *Educational assessment and reporting: A new approach*. Sydney: Harcourt Brace Jovanovich.

Johnston, P. (1989). Constructive evaluation and the improvement of teaching and learning! *Teachers College Record, 90*(4).

Kemp, M. (1989). The holistic classroom: Assessment of children with special needs. In E. Daly (Ed.), *Monitoring children's language development*. Melbourne: Australian Reading Association.

Kletzien, S.B., & Bednar, M.R. (1990). Dynamic assessment for at-risk readers! *Journal of Reading, 33*, 528–533.

Law, B. (1984). *Uses and abuses of profiling*. London: Harper & Row. Quoted in Broadfoot, op. cit.

Mossenson, L., Hill, P., & Masters, G. (1987). *Tests of Reading Comprehension (TORCH) manual*. Melbourne: ACER.

School Programs Division, Ministry of Education and Training, Victoria. (1991). *English profiles handbook: Assessing and reporting students' progress in English*. Melbourne: Education Shop, Ministry of Education and Training, Victoria.

Tuinman, J. Jaap. (1986). Reading is recognition when reading is not reasoning! In S. De Castell, A. Luke, & K. Egan. *Literacy, society and schooling: A reader*. Cambridge: Cambridge University Press.

*Reading assessment options
for teachers of junior
secondary students*
117

Graded self assessment

Kaye Lowe

I am not a teacher: only a fellow traveller of whom you asked the way. I pointed ahead—ahead of myself as well as you. *George Bernard Shaw*

This is a powerful statement about evaluation and one that reflects what I observed taking place in Jeff Newtown's Virginian classrooms in the US. So moved was I by what I witnessed that I was left wondering why the rest of the world was still worrying about a solution to improve grammar and the next set of test questions? Rarely in my twenty years of observing in classrooms have I seen the passion, respect, and desire to learn as evidenced in these Senior English classes.

On one occasion, I observed a mixed ability class celebrate poems crafted from lived experiences. The students wrote so poignantly that their courage to share left me with goose bumps. Why were these students willing to really stretch out to embrace literacy? Why did they use writing as a means to discovering themselves? Why did Scott, a college-bound student, report that the most memorable experience in his school career was the day Abe, the least academically gifted student, shared a poem with the class?

In Jeff's classrooms, students are central to the curriculum. Assessment is not something done to them. Learners' self knowledge is what counts and as Jeff explains, "I was moved to teach students how to know when they had delivered the goods."

These students do not write cute responses to teacher's prompts—they write from their realities, about heartfelt experiences; experiences that often remain without an audience because they fear their writing will not be taken seriously. They share books and talk about authors with the same fervour and I wonder why this is the exception and not the norm. Maybe as teachers, we have focused so much on the minors that the fundamental passion for learning has been sabotaged by a system that prioritises fiddling with the constraints of language in order to be right, rather than literate. These students desire to succeed, to be passionate and interested in learning, and to be acknowledged for who it is they strive to become.

From *Literacy Learning: The Middle Years*, 8(1), February 2000. Reprinted with permission of the Australian Literacy Educators' Association.

While secondary education remains locked within the narrow confines of what it means to be a reader and writer, student potential remains tethered to the past. Little has changed in secondary education over the last 30 years and the incidence of aliteracy continues to increase. In contrast, the 1200 student evaluations of Jeff's English classes, collected over a four year period, reveal that these students are aware that the power of literacy has transformed their lives. However, focusing on real reading, writing, listening, and speaking may be too simple a solution to our ever-prominent literacy woes.

Basic principles of learning and teaching

In Jeff's classrooms there are a number of principles that drive learning and teaching.

A question of trust

Fundamental to all that happens in these classrooms is the belief that students desire to learn when they control their reading and writing and are trusted to know and monitor their progress. Jeff's classrooms mirror how we operate in real life as opposed to school life. Relationships built on trust and respect drive how learning is done. He trusts that those doing the learning can make judgements about how well it is done. If we expect learners to make decisions about the quality of their efforts, they need to be given power and responsibility to do so. The students contend:

> It is harder because we have to be honest with ourselves and know that what we get is what we deserve.

> It [self assessment] lets our conscience take over and lets us be honest with ourselves.

When students talk about assessment, they share that it has little to do with grades and a lot to do with being honest. They describe assessment in terms of outcomes for learning: "He is trying to make the classroom a co-operative effort between teachers and students to increase learning."

Respect, trust, and relationships

Words such as "cares," "fair," "trusts," "responsibility," "involved," "respect," "treats us like adults" are used by the students to describe their relationship with the teacher. They recognise that the expectation is to be adult in their approach and to take responsibility for learning. "You give us the same adult respect you wish should be given to you."

Students appreciate that their opinions are valued and that they are heard. "You actually wanted our opinions and that shocked me. Most teachers do not," and "He believes and has confidence in our learning ability and wants us to be independent."

A safe learning environment

A feeling of security and enjoyment is crucial to these classrooms. "I will remember the feeling of security...I will remember reading more than I ever have." A reluctant reader explains: "In ten years' time, I will remember the first time I read out loud in front of everyone." There is a real sense that "we are in this together" and learning is to be gratifying.

In terms of enjoyment, Thomas paints a graphic picture of his discovery of literature: "I will always remember how you showed me what reading is all about. Until I started reading the Tolkien Trilogy, reading was just words on a page. You gave me a book I needed to read and I got to watch a full length movie in technicolour in the back of my head."

Link learning and assessment

Together learning and assessment inform curriculum. Students do not write for a grade, they write because they are learners with something to say and they trust the support of an appreciative audience with whom they celebrate. In these classrooms, learning is not a performance for the grade-assigning teacher, it is about gaining new understandings and insights. As explained by one student: "I figured out that he knows that students actually learn by writing self assessments. He taught us how to think."

The process is made explicit

The assessment criteria

The process is simple. Students know what is being assessed and why. They are aware of the criteria by which grades are assigned and they know that there is flexibility within the model to adjust and modify their grade. They document their reading, writing, and class participation every six weeks. Students outline the process: "I lay everything out in front of me and then I read back through the syllabus to check everything off. I look at the grades I got for the assignments completed." Another student claims: "It gives the student a chance to lay out what they have done and actually see what they deserve. There is no mystery to how the grade is determined," and "You know what you are going to get before you get it."

The syllabus

The syllabus outlines the specific components to be completed. Basically, each syllabus has specific tasks assigned according to reading, writing, and class participation. The components vary according to the time of the year, observations of students, their capabilities, interests, and external factors, for example, scheduled productions. In determining the first six week syllabus, the results of a spelling inventory, oral reading assessment, and a writing sample are taken into consideration and these are used by Jeff as a baseline to guide curriculum choices.

The object of the first six weeks is to get to know the students. What is offered in subsequent syllabi is the result of ongoing observations and negotiations with students. Jeff explains: "The six weeks timeframe and the SOLs (Standards of Learning) do not determine nor restrict what I do with my classes. My intention is to get there one six-weeks at a time. The tendency each year has been to move more and more into workshops and the students complete less and less in common."

In order to self assess reading, writing, and class participation, a number of methods are used, including lit letters, reading logs, and class participation summary statements. In addition, grades are assigned by Jeff for specific writing tasks outlined in the syllabus. Students are responsible for keeping track of their reading and writing grades.

1. Lit letters.   Using a letter format, students write a one-page letter about their self-selected book(s). In the lit letters students enter into thought-provoking conversations about books read. The guidelines ask students to reflect on what they have read.

Jeff replies and his responses are usually in terms of goal setting. For example, "Have you considered *Catcher in the Rye?*; books by Paulson; I will suggest lots of books, you'll discard most of them, pick a few to try and see if any grab you." Jeff explains:

> I write more to these students than perhaps any other teacher they have
> ever experienced. It is a huge commitment in time but it is so valuable. It
> is the essence of what I do. It is how I win them over. They can't deny that
> I know them and these responses are a sound basis to our intellectual
> discussions. The response is always on a personal level.

Lit letters are also used as the basis of small-group discussions, mini-lessons, and teacher demonstrations. Lit letters are submitted on a regular basis, usually every two weeks.

2. Reading logs. Students maintain reading logs. When they complete their self assessment, they are requested to review their logs in terms of variety, breadth, depth, quantity. Students are expected to read a range of texts and read for a minimum of half-an-hour a day.

Jeff has a very practical approach to calculating the minimum number of pages to be read in a six-week period. Students are asked to read silently a self-selected book during class-time for ten minutes. They then count the number of pages read, multiply the number by three (making the equivalent of one half-hour), and then by five school days and by six school weeks. Generally, students agree that reading 600 pages every six weeks is not an unrealistic expectation based on this formula.

In addition to the number of pages required, students are expected to read across a range of genres. An extensive paperback library is available in the classroom. Jeff explains how he guides the students' choices:

> I guide students to sample a range of text types. I might suggest that a student read an escapist and interpretive text during a six-week period. Just as it would be extremely rude to make disparaging remarks about a friend's choice of a book, it would be beyond reproach to do it to students. Students do not recover from such an experience. I make a wide selection of books available and students get to choose at their level. I support the more reluctant readers in baby steps towards becoming good readers.

3. Class participation. The rules for class participation are made explicit and simple.

- SSR (sustained silent reading) occurs on a daily basis for half-an-hour. It is taken seriously and talking and sleeping are banned.
- During author's circles, students who do not come to class with draft response papers to share are asked to leave the circle until the work is done.
- Assignments are due on time.

According to Jeff: "You can't fail class participation unless you try really hard. If we apply the notion of being a literacy club, it is impossible to fail the club unless you cease being a member and students have to take responsibility for making that decision."

Student assessment

At the conclusion of a six-week period, the syllabus is reviewed in class. Together, Jeff and the students outline what has been completed on easel paper. The outline is then used as a guide by the students to compose their self assessment letter. They reflect on and analyse what they have achieved. A short summary statement is completed and a student assessment (SA) grade is faintly recorded on the back of the summary statement. Grades are on the scale of A for superior, B above average, C average, D below average, and E fail—students agree that they have experienced years of having grades imposed on them and that they know what an A looks like.

Teacher assessment

The statements are collected and read. Jeff reflects on his "holistic impressions" of the students' achievements, the work submitted, and the students' personal reflections. "I sit down with my grade book, total up points for graded essays, and reflect on what I have observed about each student during the six-week period. I ask myself questions such as: Did Steve use SSR well? Didn't John bring in the article that had an example of parallelism in the lead?"

Again, he considers the variety, breadth, depth, and quantity of texts read. Graded essays are looked at in terms of writing performance and class participation is considered in terms of effort. After reading and reflecting on each summary statement, Jeff assigns a teacher assessment (TA) grade at the bottom of the summary statement. He then turns the statement over to see if there is a match between the teacher TA and SA. If the two correspond, the grade is awarded. The grade is circled to indicate that "this grade is going to the book." When the TA and SA correspond, there is obvious agreement about the quality of work being produced and teacher comments are kept to a minimum, for example, "great work," "keep on reading."

Talk to the grade: Sorting out discrepancies

When there is a mismatch between the TA and SA, the teacher and student "talk to the grade" and a compromise is reached. On returning the summary statements and grades, Jeff informs the class: "'If you have a concern about your grade, I am prepared to stop five minutes before class finishes today to discuss it with you. If you are happy with the grade you have been given then turn it over and it will be collected.' This way I know that they are not harbouring any resentment. The grade issue is resolved quickly and painlessly."

Students are often given the benefit of the doubt the first time there is a mismatch. Jeff describes the process: "For example, if in the first six weeks, Dwayne gives himself a SA of A and he receives TA of B. I say, I will go with an A this time but I think you can read more, show me that you deserve this A and read like the demon this next six weeks." In subsequent grading periods, Jeff's comments may be different: "I'm going with my grade this time because you have not read as much as the last six weeks. I'd like to help you find some books that will grab you, then you will have no trouble reading lots of pages."

In cases where students experience mismatches, their reflections are not condemning or negative. With traditional assessment the student often looks to blame the teacher for the poor result, and the distinction between failing work and failing as a learner is not made. These students recognise the difference: "A student learns nothing from just receiving a bad mark from a teacher except to despise the teacher." The uncertainties and ambiguities surrounding traditional assessment practices are identified: "We usually never understand the grade we get and now it is us who decides and now we know why we get the grade we do." They recognise the mystery of teacher-assigned grades when the learner is left out of the process: "Most teachers don't show how they graded. At the end of six weeks, you get to come up and look at your grade and that's what you get," and "What is the difference between a 93 and a 94?" With graded self assessment, students look at the mismatch in terms of what they learned about themselves. "I learned when it comes right down to it, I'm not very certain about myself and my work."

On the other hand, when the TA is less than the SA, students appreciate knowing that they can negotiate.

> If you give us something other than what we think we deserve, we can put a higher grade and you will take another look.
>
> You actually get to step up and voice what you thought you should be getting whereas in other classes it is all up to the teacher.

Confrontations and ill feelings are eliminated. In the twelve hundred responses, there is no evidence of hostility or sense that the students have been deceived.

Does it work?

There is a consistently high correlation, evident over a four-year period, between the TA and SA grades. According to Jeff:

Students assign themselves D's and E's when they know that they have not delivered the goods. They under-rate themselves, they identify how they will make amends for giving themselves a poor grade and they acknowledge their efforts when they have worked hard.

The high correlation between teacher-assigned grades and student-assigned grades is an indication that students when trusted, show they are trustworthy. A student explained his understanding of the process, "Students know that what is at stake is not a grade, but their honesty. They know that the teacher is very well aware of the progress they make. He knows what they read because he asks them and they document what they do—the teacher and the students have the documentary evidence."

The outcome of graded self assessment is learning, not the assigning of a grade. Graded self assessment puts decision-making and responsibility back into the hands of those responsible for completing the tasks. Students frequently highlight their role in the process—"A grade is no longer given to you by your teacher, it is earned," and "It lets you know that it is definitely our responsibility to learn and Mr. Newton is here to help in the process. He seems less of a teacher and more of a learner-helper." The authority of teacher and student become obscure—"It kind of reversed the roles of student and teacher for a few minutes."

Students frequently comment on how they use self assessment as a springboard for goal-setting for the next six week period. They become self-regulating.

> I got my head out of the clouds and put it to work.
>
> After seeing how I did one six weeks, it makes me want to try harder the next six weeks, so that I stay consistent.

Students receive regular and timely feedback on their learning rather than being left to suffer the consequences of imposed assessment with little scope to change the outcome.

Assessment is an emotive issue and most teachers suffer through the grading period. A myriad of controversial questions surround the traditional assessment process:

> How do you rank a student's effort and how do you know what effort looks like?
>
> Do we grade progress or achievement?
>
> How do we compare the grades of the student who came into a class with very little knowledge and learned a lot, compared to the student who came into the classroom knowing a lot but learned very little?

Graded self assessment can eliminate these tedious and frustrating concerns.

Monitoring the quality of their work

Students recognise and acknowledge the quality of their efforts. They reflect on both positive and negative aspects of work completed and the process of learning.

> I see on plain paper how hard I worked and the quality of the work that I did. I realised for the most part I am a self-motivated learner.
> I pretty much do what is required of me and a lot of times I go beyond the call of duty.

Others draw attention to their lack of effort.

> I realised that sometimes I am wrong about my participation.
> ...my grade stayed at D or C this year basically I did not read a lot of pages for you but I thought I read a lot for myself.
> I learned that is hard to admit that I am lazy and haven't done my best work.

Despite the fact that this student gave himself C's and D's, he claims to have really enjoyed the classes and learned a lot. There is no animosity in his response because he fully realises that responsibility rests with him.

Students appreciate the benefits of monitoring their efforts. They acknowledge the value of organisational skills and responsibility.

> I learned that I could keep myself on pace and on task better
> I learned to budget time for my projects.
> My reading got better because I kept track of it.

Students also appreciate that the teacher has input into the negotiation of a grade—not as the final arbitrator but as someone who brings another perspective to their learning. As a student recalls: "I told you what I deserve and you told me what I deserve and we compromised, but at least I had a say in the matter."

Resetting their internal thermostat—redefining potential because someone keeps asking

Students rarely, if ever, discuss their grades with their peers. They are adamant that comparing grades is of little value when the grade is a statement about their honesty. "I don't talk about it because I realise what I have done and if I give myself an A it has nothing to do with what others give themselves. It is because I have done the work well during the six weeks," and "It is a grade between me and the teacher about how well I have done," and "It is about me and only I can judge how well I have done."

When students reflect on their achievement, they interrogate their learning and make plans to improve.

> I learned that I am a slow reader and need to read a lot more to become a better reader.
>
> I learned that I procrastinate a whole lot. It really helped me to stay on track and when I fell behind I knew exactly why.
>
> I surprised myself, I did not think I could read that fast.

Acknowledgement for work effort is intrinsic. Students value learning. "I learned to give myself credit when I deserve it. I had better self-confidence because I had a goal to reach by the end of the six weeks." The privilege of being successful is not limited to the top 5% but opened to all learners responsible for monitoring their achievements rather than be reminded of their failures. As assessment is regarded as an individual concern, students respect that all learners learn at different paces and in different ways.

What happens in these classrooms is an enriching, life-altering experience. It is about human endeavour and success at all levels. I was hooked on their passion. I witnessed their drive to learn and Jeff's enthusiasm to teach. When Frances anticipates what she will remember in ten years time about these classes, I endorse her response. "I will remember what it was like to be...special."

Testing times for literacy?

Brian Cambourne

It's now five years since the Basic Skills Tests in Literacy were introduced in New South Wales. Their introduction in 1988 by the newly elected State government seemed to have a strong mandate from the electorate, and as a consequence, five cohorts of grades 3 and 6 state school children have been given the test. Furthermore, there has been strong pressure from within some of the private sectors of the education system (in particular the Catholic system) for the same or similar kinds of tests to be introduced.

It is significant that in the five years that they have been used the tests have been favourably received by the majority of the electorate, so much so that legislation has been passed which ensures that the tests will remain an annual event. It is unlikely that a change of government will repeal this legislation. It is my belief that we are witnessing the beginnings of a movement towards regular state-wide (possibly nation-wide) accountability testing similar to that which is presently flourishing in most parts of the United States.

There are some aspects of this movement in the United States which should concern us. It is my opinion that there are serious inconsistencies with respect to the assumptions that the U.S. testing industry has made about literacy and assessment, and as a consequence the instruments which they have developed are, in my opinion, flawed and atheoretical. Given this opinion, I believe that it is important that we look closely at the instruments which are being used in our own country. We need to be fully informed and aware if we are to resist the negative outcomes that can result from such a movement.

Although the NSW Basic Skills Tests have some innovative surface features (e.g., a magazine format), at a deeper level they have many of the features of traditional measurement-based tests which are used in the United States. Like the majority of instruments used in the United States, the NSW Basic Skills Tests are group administered, standardised (both at the level of administration and interpretation of results), comparative (i.e., norm referenced), and product oriented. While these similarities are important, of greater significance is the fact that the tests also reflect the same underlying assumptions. These assumptions are:

From *The Australian Journal of Language and Literacy*, 15(4), November 1992. Reprinted with permission of the Australian Literacy Educators' Association.

- Assessment is synonymous with measurement.
- Assessment must be objective.
- Test results generated in a standardised, controlled context can be generalised to the real world.
- Process plays a minimal part in the effective performance of literacy related behaviours.
- Results from such accountability tests are both useful to, and used by, teachers and learners.

It is important that each one of these assumptions is examined in more depth.

Assessment is synonymous with measurement

This notion has had a long history in psychology and education. Binet published his first test in 1904. By 1945 Hildreth could list over 5,000 mental tests and rating scales in her bibliography (Hildreth, 1945). Somehow during this period the notions of measurement, assessment, and evaluation merged, overlapped, and in education and psychology, ultimately came to mean the same thing. If one reads back through the literature of educational and psychometric evaluation these terms were constantly juxtaposed, with measurement coming first, e.g., "measurement and evaluation," as if it had top billing. Behind this measurement oriented view of assessment there are several assumptions about literacy and literacy development which I believe are flawed.

Let me elaborate on these flaws.

Firstly, a measurement view of assessment assumes that literacy is a single, monolithic, or concrete entity similar to the amount of water in a container or the amount of gas in a cylinder. A variation of this assumption is that literacy is a single ability or skill similar to typing or using a calculator. The underlying metaphor is one of different containers (learners) being filled with differing amounts of stuff-like material (literacy).

Secondly, it assumes that basic units of this "stuff" (or skill) can be identified and quantified in much the same way as units of length and mass can be identified and quantified. To think of literacy in this way is to fall victim to what philosophers refer to as the fallacy of misplaced concreteness, i.e., fallaciously referring to something which is complex and abstract as if it were "thing-like" or concrete. The history of psychology is littered with examples of such fallacies, for example, "aggression," "intelligence," "motivation," "anxiety," to name a few.

Neither of these assumptions stands up to rigorous scrutiny.

Literacy is not a monolithic entity which is possessed in varying degrees by different people. It is a term which describes a whole collection of behaviours, skills, knowledge, processes, and attitudes. It has something to do with our ability to use language in our negotiations with the world. Often these negotiations are motivated by our desires to manipulate the world for our own benefit. Reading and writing are two linguistic ways of conducting these negotiations. So are talking, listening, thinking, reflecting, and a host of other behaviours related to cognition and critical thinking. All of these, and possibly many more make up what constitutes literate behaviour. To assume that we can capture the degree to which all four of these are possessed (or not possessed) in a unidimensional quantitative score (i.e., a number) of some kind, is simplistic in the extreme. Furthermore the assumption that units of literacy behaviour (a metre of literacy? a kilowatt? an erg?) can be identified is even more simplistic. At the core of all literate behaviour is the construction of meaning. What is the basic unit of meaning? Philosophers of language have been arguing about this and related issues since the time of Aristotle at least, and without much success.

Assessment must be objective

Society has been subtly indoctrinated over the years that the "truth" can only be arrived at through carefully controlled, detached objectivity. The stereotype of the cool, detached, objective scientist, unemotionally and "scientifically" collecting and then weighing the evidence, is one with which we are all familiar. The attainment of this kind of objectivity is enhanced (so the argument goes) if the degree to which the investigator (i.e., the scientist) actually influences the outcomes of what he or she is researching is reduced as close to zero as possible. In the jargon of research design this is called "reducing the reactivity of the subjects." This notion of objectivity has spilled over into the assessment field, partly as a result of the view of science which has been carefully promulgated over the years, and partly as a consequence of the belief that accurate measurement is at the core of any scientific enterprise. In the assessment field this lust for objectivity is allegedly achieved by interposing some objective instrument (a test) between the tester and testee and then standardising the procedures of administration and interpretation. By doing this it is claimed that any prejudices or biases which the investigator might have will be eliminated and thus the desired degrees of objectivity will be achieved.

Such claims simply do not stand up to scrutiny.

While certain "safeguards" like standardising the tester—testee relationship and context may reduce this interactivity between the tester and testee, interactivity itself can never be eliminated. Despite all the controls, a large amount will always remain, and it is not only fruitless to pretend that it is not there, it is also intellectually dishonest. Even under the most rigorous of standardisation procedures which have been most scrupulously applied, the questions on any test are, after all, posed by test designers in accordance with some perspective they hold, and that perspective includes all the biases and prejudices that normally characterise them. But it doesn't stop here. Test designers can never assume that subjects will interpret the items on any test exactly as they intended. Nor is there any guarantee that when test designers come to interpret the responses they will interpret these responses exactly as the respondents intended. Value-free, context-independent objectivity is a chimera that psychometricians have been chasing unsuccessfully since the measurement movement began. The issue of objectivity in all human research activities (and testing is after all merely one of a number of possible forms of research activity) is summed up by this observation:

> There is no guarantee that when information is collected from human subjects, by whatever method, that there will not be interaction between those subjects and the minds that determined what information to collect and how to collect it. (Krathwol, cited by Guba & Lincoln, 1981, p. 90)

Does it really matter? We need to ask whether or not assessor—assessee interaction is such a bad thing anyway, particularly with respect to the assessment of learning of something as complex and multi-dimensional as language and literacy. There is plenty of evidence to show that humans can be sensitive, reliable, trustworthy, credible instruments of data collection.

Let us consider what it is that the human-as-instrument can do that the test cannot do. Firstly, the human is a responsive instrument. It can respond to all the personal and environmental cues which exist in the assessment context. Secondly, it is adaptable. It can collect information about multiple factors at multiple levels, simultaneously. Thirdly, it is "smart." Like a "smart bomb" it can hone in on information, change direction, run down leads, follow a trail, and ultimately hit the target. It can clarify, process, explore, summarise, triangulate on the spot, and do a host of other things that standardised instruments could never do. In short it can cope with complexities much more effectively and quickly than any standardised test.

It would seem that the complex nature of language behaviour demands an instrument which can cope with such complexity. Currently, the only instrument capable of doing all these things is the human mind. Rather than avoiding the interactions which subjects and assessors are prone to, we should be exploiting them and maximising the richness and quality of data they can generate. Subjectivity as a source of bias and prejudice becomes a non-issue when rigorous and appropriate credibility procedures are used.

Test results generated in a standardised, controlled context can be generalised to the real world

There is a widely held notion that scores on tests of reading, writing, language, and so on, which are administered and interpreted under standardised conditions, reflect the reading and writing behaviours which occur in the real world. At least that is what one could infer from the way that such scores are used. Although widely held, this notion is difficult to sustain, because it too is based on some rather dubious assumptions. Let us explore what some of these are:

One is that the highly unusual context of the standardised test does not affect the performance of readers, writers, or talkers placed in that context. Another is that the standardised context will be similarly interpreted by those experiencing it. Yet another is that the behaviours which are brought to bear in the contrived testing situation comprise an accurate model of those used in everyday circumstances. There are multiple examples in the literature which unequivocally deny the validity of these assumptions.

Here is one from my own experience.

The case of Anne

Some years ago I completed a rather large research project. The research question I set out to address was: "When children first enter the school system, what language abilities do they bring with them?"

I decided to use two very different data collection methods. Firstly, I decided to use a highly reputable standardised test, the ITPA, to tap into my subjects' language know-how. Secondly, I decided to devise a way of spying on these children using an unobtrusive radio microphone, "bug," to tap into their language as they used it in natural conditions. In those days I was even more naive than I am now and I thought that both sets of data would help me get a good accurate fix on the answer to the question.

Imagine my surprise when I discovered that both sets of data were contradictory. When I looked at the individual scores on the ITPA and compared them with what the naturalistic data showed, it was as though I was looking at two different groups of language-users. Here is an example of what I mean.

Anne, whose chronological age at the time of testing was 5 years 9 months, achieved a raw score of 12 on the sub-test labelled "Auditory Reception." This gave her an "Auditory Reception Age" of 3 years 10 months (nearly two years below her chronological age), and a scale score of 25 (almost two standard deviations below the norm). According to the test designers this sub-test assessed the ability of the child "to derive meaning from verbally presented material" (Kirk, McCarthy, & Kirk, 1968, p. 9).

The test consists of questions such as "Do dogs eat?" "Do trees fly?" to which the subject is merely required to indicate "yes" or "no." Anne failed miserably on this test, missing questions like "Do people marry?" and "Do ants crawl?" From the point of view of the standardised interpretative procedures of the ITPA, such a poor result would be interpreted to mean that Anne had inadequate control of vocabulary, or that she used faulty listening strategies, or that she had some problems integrating what she heard with what she knew, or all three. Some ITPA experts (and I considered myself one in those days) would also claim that she had not yet acquired the concepts and meanings underlying "people marrying" or "ants crawling."

However when I analysed the transcripts of Anne's verbal behaviour I found that in four hours of continuous interaction with parents, peers, teachers, and neighbours, Anne had been involved in hundreds of verbal exchanges which contained thousands of sentences and tens of thousands of words about a multitude of topics. In all these data, using the most flexible of criteria, there is not one instance of her ever failing "to derive the intended meaning from verbally presented material."

In other words, in the natural situation Anne did not fail one of the thousands of auditory reception tasks that the world threw up to her. Furthermore, there were at least two instances where she gave evidence that she fully understood the vocabulary and concepts involved in two of the items she failed. In one instance she discussed her cousin's forthcoming marriage ceremony. There was no doubt that she fully appreciated and understood that people DO marry. In another instance she called a friend over to observe ants crawling on an ant hill in the play ground. To assert that she failed to give the correct response to the question "Do ants crawl?" because she does not know what ants are or what it means to crawl, or the fact that when ants move it can be described as "crawling," is simply not defensible.

This intrigued me and I went back through every subject's response to the many items on the ITPA and compared it with what the language collected under natural conditions revealed. Anne was not an isolated example. There were other similar discrepancies sprinkled regularly throughout the data. Since that experience I've encountered the same phenomenon many times. The assumption that a measurement-based, traditional, standardised test can validly capture the amount of language or literacy that one possesses in all contexts is difficult to sustain.

Process plays a minimal part in the effective performance of literacy related behaviours

The emphasis in measurement-based assessment procedures is on outcomes or "product." What the assessor takes away from the testing context is the end result of what the learner thought, knew, and did during the testing period. Usually this product takes the form of sheets which have marks in boxes, words in slots, or sentences in spaces. In some instances it can be in the form of sustained written discourse (like the traditional end of semester written examination). This emphasis suggests one of two things:

(i) the test makers and test givers assume that the processes by which these products were created are not vital factors in the enterprise, or,

(ii) they assume that the processes which were used to create the product can be inferred from an examination of it alone.

Neither of these assumptions stands up to scrutiny.

What research has taught us about reading and writing in the last twenty years is at variance with both of these assumptions. A most important form of information which we can get about a pupil's literacy learning is process information (i.e., information which describes how the literacy act was performed and the reasons why it was performed in that way). With respect to reading, for example, it is important to know not only the degree to which the text was understood (i.e., the end "product"), but how readers arrived at whatever meanings they happen to construct. It is imperative to know whether readers predict, what the basis of these predictions are, what strategies they use when blocked, whether they self-correct, what triggers these self corrections, and so on.

The same principles hold for the assessment of writing. Research in the last decade has conclusively shown that effective writers, and effective users of writing, employ a range of strategies (processes) that help them get from blank page to finished product. They have strategies for getting ideas, finding information, improving their meanings, getting over blocks, getting response to their developing pieces, dealing with conventions, setting out, going public, and so on. My own research over the last few years has shown that effective readers and writers are also extremely confident (to the point of arrogance!), have high degrees of what we call "meta-textual aware-ness" (i.e., conscious awareness of the processes they use, the knowledge they use, and the connections between them), and readily use reading and writing to help them solve their learning problems because they enjoy en-gaging in both (Cambourne, 1988). Surely these could also be considered to be critical indicators of language growth? How does one find out about these things from a standardised reading test or from a piece of writing pro-duced under examination conditions?

What about the assumption that process can be inferred from product? There is a strong consensus that it simply isn't possible. As Donald Murray pointed out, "Process cannot be inferred from product anymore than a pig can be inferred from a sausage" (Murray, 1982, p. 18). Goodman's work into miscue analysis has shown this with respect to reading as well.

The dangers of assuming that product could reveal process was painfully driven home to me in 1981 (Cambourne, 1981). I had completed a rather large study on the use of cloze procedure as an instrument to as-sess reading ability. At the time I was infatuated with cloze procedure. I thought it was the answer to all of our assessment dilemmas. At that time I believed that it tapped into silent reading behaviour. I also believed that its focus was comprehension. Furthermore, by adapting some of Ken Goodman's miscue taxonomy to the "Not-Exact-Replacements" (NERs) I believed it was possible to get insights into the underlying processes which readers were using. As well as all this it could be administered on a group basis, marked by computer, and would give a numerical score, and a diag-nosis. No wonder I was besotted with it! I therefore decided to research it carefully to prove that my infatuation was well founded. In this study I carefully observed and questioned readers as they completed cloze type tasks to find out how they did it.

One of the chilling things I discovered was that ineffective readers could put the correct word in the slot for the wrong reasons. Instead of working out what the appropriate word was as they were supposed to (i.e., by cu-mulatively building up the story line and holding it in mind while they test-ed semantic and syntactic options) they would (cognitively) "grab" at the word either side of the slot on the basis of minimal syntactic cues and word association, and "fluke" the correct word on enough occasions to lift their scores significantly, or they would fill in the blanks in reverse or random order. It was chilling because in the year before I had helped a local school grade all its pupils into reading groups on the basis of such a procedure. I'd convinced the staff that cloze was a much more valid means of tapping into comprehension than more traditional types of assessment, and that it also simulated the silent reading process they would normally engage in. I still have strong twinges of conscience about that experience.

Any assessment procedure which fails to take account of process must result in inaccurate and untrustworthy assessment data.

Results from accountability tests are both useful to, and used by, teachers and learners

Will teachers use the information provided by standardised accountability tests? "Usability" is, after all, one of the basic criteria used when evaluating tests (Gronlund, 1976). Research which specifically addresses this question is quite conclusive: The majority of teachers do not use the information provided by standardised tests (Boyd et al., 1975; Door-Bremme, 1982).

A related question which could be asked is, "Can teachers in fact use accountability test information to support their teaching and their students' learning?" The answer to this question is more complex. It could be argued that using a test to hold someone publicly accountable is a potentially ego-threatening enterprise. The tester becomes "the enemy" and the aim of those being tested is to conceal their weaknesses, or at least prevent them from being detected. This conflicts with the notion that for assessment to be a useful adjunct of instruction it is essential that weaknesses and deficiencies be personally confronted and dealt with in a non-threatening, supportive, tutorial-like context, in which the expert responds to and thus informs the novice. At least this is how powerful and permanent learning occurs in the real world (i.e., learning to talk). There is a conflict of purposes here which to my mind is irreconcilable. The use of the same tests for both accountability and instructional purposes seems to be a logical impossibility.

There are some other assumptions about accountability testing's value as an insurance for quality learning with which I have difficulty. It assumes, for example, that teachers are willing and able to change their teaching behaviour on the basis of information which tells them that last year's class did not perform as well as other students of the same grade level. This assumption needs to be tested. Although I have no direct evidence, the work that some of us completed a few years ago into the impact of ELIC in NSW has led us into the area of teacher change (Cambourne et al., 1987). Our recent data indicate that teachers will not change their behaviour unless they first change their theories and belief systems (Turbill, 1992). Two factors seem to effect this kind of change. One is time (up to 18 months), the other is information which is contextually relevant, such as, what is happening with respect to their pupils in the busy ebb and flow of the daily grind in the classes they happen to be teaching now. I find it difficult to concede that scores on a standardised test from a class taught the year before have the same potential for bringing about similar kinds of changes.

There is another less visible assumption which concerns me a great deal. Accountability testing assumes that teaching and learning are basically unenjoyable activities, and therefore teachers and pupils need to be given "something to work for." This in turn leads to the notion that learning is "work" (and that activities that need to be engaged in must therefore be meaningless and trivial). This stance denies everything we know about the relationship between intrinsic and extrinsic motivation (i.e., that over time extrinsic motivation successfully extinguishes any intrinsic motivation which might have been initially present, and that extrinsically motivated behaviours are not durable).

If accountability testing using measurement-based theory is here to stay, what can we do?

If we agree that a view of assessment which is based on a measurement metaphor is underpinned by a set of assumptions which are atheoretical and flawed, what can be done about it?

I think it would help if the public recognised these flaws and in turn became more critical of the assessment devices and the industry responsible for them, and less critical of its teachers. In order to do this the public has to be made aware of a whole new approach to learning, language, literacy, and the assessment of them. It then has to be prepared to accept a much less formal, quantitative approach to assessment, and replace it with a more qualitative, seemingly less formal approach (N.B. emphasis on "seemingly"). In other words it has to be made aware of the paradigm shift that is occurring, not only in education but in other sciences as well. Unfortunately, given the current political climate, it seems unlikely that the public will readily accept such a change. It would simply be viewed as a ploy to avoid being accountable. Notwithstanding this, I don't think we have any option but to help the public understand, and in order to do this we have to educate its members, and win their trust.

How do we do this? There's no one sure-fire recipe which I can offer. There are some tentative principles which I think can be kept in mind.

1. Never argue against accountability testing, per se. Merely argue against the kind of accountability testing which is used. Begin to support accountability testing if it uses procedures and techniques which optimise learning for all.

2. Insist that the major goal of any kind of assessment, the bottom line so to speak, must be optimal learning for all. It is difficult not to agree with such a goal. Given what we know about language and learning it is also difficult to explain how measurement-based accountability tests used in isolation contribute to the achievement of optimum learning for all.

3. Provide an acceptable alternative. Develop some assessment procedures which will show how well children are performing in much more meaningful, rich, and useful ways.

My concern is that if we don't begin this process of public education we could quickly proceed down the same path that the USA has gone. Frank Smith, in his book *Insult to Intelligence* (1986), paints a depressing picture of the stranglehold that accountability testing has on the education of American children. Smith begins this description with a quote from another writer:

> ...Karp summarises: "From first grade to the twelfth, from one coast to another, instruction in America's classrooms is almost entirely dogmatic. Answers are right and answers are wrong, but mostly answers are short...important decisions are based on test scores...teachers are more likely to teach to the tests and less likely to bother with non-tested activities, such as writing, speaking, problem solving, or the real reading of real books...." The short right answer has come to dominate education, but only because of the mania for teaching and testing by the most mechanical means possible "objectively." The theory is that to teach and evaluate learning in any way except by numbers would be unscientific and unreliable, and to allow scores or grades to be allocated on the basis of personal judgement would be "subjective" (a perjorative term) and biased. Ironically, the endeavour to remove the personal and possibly prejudicial from educational evaluation has resulted in the totally arbitrary and distorted procedure of teaching and testing only those things which can be cleanly scored right or wrong and counted. The cost of removing human error has been the removal of all humanity and the reduction of education to trivia. (Smith, 1986, pp. 135–136)

REFERENCES

Boyd, J., McKenna, B.H., Stake, R.H., & Yashinsky, J. (1975). *A study of testing practices in the Royal Oak (Michigan) public schools.* Royal Oak, MI: Royal Oak City School District. (ERIC No. ED 117161)

Cambourne, B.L. (1981). *Coping with cloze.* Paper delivered at First South Pacific Reading Conference, Auckland, New Zealand.

Cambourne, B.L., Turbill, J., Keeble, P.J., Ferguson, B., & Colvin, R. (1987). *N.S.W. evaluation of the early literacy in-service course: Progress report December 1986*. Centre for Studies in Literacy, University of Wollongong, New South Wales, Australia.

Cambourne, B.L. (1988). *What research has taught us about writing*. Paper presented at the Second Writing in Australia Conference, Kuringai College, Sydney.

Door-Bremme, D. (1982). *Assessing students: Teachers' routine practices and reasoning* (CSE Report no. 194). Los Angeles: Centre For Study in Evaluation.

Gronlund, N.E. (1976). *Measurement and evaluation in teaching* (3rd ed.). New York: Macmillan.

Guba, E., & Lincoln, Y. (1981). *Effective evaluation: Improving the usefulness of evaluation results through responsive and naturalistic approaches*. San Francisco: Jossey Bass.

Hildreth, G.H. (1945). *A bibliography of mental tests and rating scales* (Supplement to 2nd ed.). New York: Psychological Corporation.

Kirk, S.A., McCarthy, J.J., & Kirk, W.D. (1968). *Illinois test of psycholinquistic abilities*. (Revised Edition). Urbana, IL: University of Illinois.

Murray, D. (1982). *Writing as process: How writing finds its own meaning. Learning by teaching*. Montclair, NJ: Boynton-Cook.

Smith, F. (1986). *Insult to intelligence: The bureaucratic invasion of our classrooms*. Portsmouth, NH: Heinemann.

Turbill, J. (1992). *The evaluation of the Frameworks program in thirty-one school districts in New York State*. Ongoing, unpublished doctoral research, Centre for Studies in Literacy, University of Wollongong, New South Wales, Australia.

What's the score on testing?

Brian Cambourne

The majority of assessment instruments currently used by education systems share the following characteristics:

- They are given only once to each pupil.
- They are given to a large group simultaneously.
- They have been/will be standardised—for both administration and interpretation of results.
- They are used to compare group with group and individual with individual.
- The interpretation of the results will be based solely on the product.
- They are marked and interpreted with computer technology.

There are five basic assumptions which underlie these kinds of assessment instruments.

1. Assessment is synonymous with testing

Tests which compare individuals and are norm-referenced are inevitably based on quantitative measurement. Measurement-oriented assessment applied to literacy assumes that:

- literacy is a single entity like a cylinder of gas or a tank filled with water
- the basic units of such an entity can be identified and measured as with, for example, litres of water.

These assumptions need to be questioned. Can something as complex as literacy be turned into one single characteristic like the volume of gas in a cylinder? (How much gas is in this cylinder? How much literacy is in

From "Looking at the Issues," *Practically Primary*, 4(1), February 1999. Reprinted with permission of the Australian Literacy Educators' Association. This is a revised version of an article published by the Australian Education Network in their 1989 publication *Testing: Tonic or Toxic?*

this child?) And is there a basic unit which has been identified? For example, a gram or a kilowatt of literacy?

2. Assessment must be objective

Over the years we have been indoctrinated that truth can be arrived at only through careful, controlled, detached objectivity. In the assessment field, this need for objectivity is achieved by placing some instrument (a test) between the tester and the testee and then standardising the procedures of administration and interpretation of the results.

However, even with the most rigorous standardised procedures it cannot be denied that:

- the test questions reflect the perspective and values of the test designer,
- test subjects do not always interpret the questions in the way intended by the test designer, and
- when marking the responses, the test designer will not necessarily interpret the answers in the way intended by the respondent.

In short, value-free, context-independent objectivity is simply not possible.

Many educators argue there is evidence to show that humans can be sensitive, reliable, trustworthy, and credible instruments of data collection and interpretation.

3. Test results generated in a standardised, controlled context can be generalised to the real world

Once-only, standardised tests of literacy assume that the scores which learners achieve reflect reading and writing behaviours which occur in the real world. However,

- how certain can one be that the highly unusual context of the standardised test will not affect the performance of readers and writers placed in that situation?
- how certain can one be that the standardised context will be similarly interpreted by all those experiencing it (for example, children from different cultural backgrounds)?

• how certain can one be that the behaviours which are brought to bear in the testing situation reflect those used in everyday circumstances?

4. Process plays a minimal part on the effective performance of literacy related behaviours

The emphasis in once-only, standardised, group-administered, norm-referenced instruments is on outcomes or product. What the assessor takes away from the testing context is the end result of what the learner thought, knew, and did during the testing period. Usually this product takes the form of test papers which have marks in boxes or bubbles, words in slots, or sentences in spaces.

Over the last thirty years research has shown that the most important information we can get about a child's literacy learning is *process information which describes how the literacy act was performed and the reasons why it was performed in that way.*

In reading, examples of such processes include predicting, constructing meanings, and self-correcting.

In writing there are generating ideas, getting over blocks, dealing with conventions, and so on. How can one find out about these things from a standardised reading test or from a piece of writing produced under exam conditions?

5. Results from such tests are both useful to, and used by, teachers and learners

It has been argued that usability ought to be the key criteria of tests and testing programs. *One needs to ask "Will teachers use the information this test will provide?"*

Research specifically addressing this question shows the majority of teachers do not themselves use such information. How the results are used and by whom, as well as why the tests were administered in the first place, are complex questions. Possible systemic uses include holding teachers accountable and selecting candidates for special groups and roles.

Unless those who wish to administer these tests can show clearly that the end result will be optimal learning for all, then widespread testing programs should be critically examined. It is difficult to show how holding teachers accountable, or how putting children into special groups, does in fact lead to optimal learning.

REFERENCES

Boyd, J., McKenna, B., Staake, R., & Yashinsky, J. (1975). *A study of testing practices in the Royal Oak Public Schools*. Royal Oak, MI: Royal Oak City School District. (ERIC No. Ed 1117161)

Door-Bremme, D. (1982). *Assessing students: Teachers' routine practices and reasoning* (CSE Report No. 194). Los Angeles: Centre for Study in Evaluation.

Gronlund, N. (1976). *Measurement and evaluation in teaching*. New York: Macmillan.

Exploring the relationship between large-scale literacy testing programs and classroom-based assessment: A focus on teachers' accounts

Claire M. Wyatt-Smith

Literacy education and its assessment are currently major concerns for government, educational professionals, and the community, with policy implications that reach beyond educational practice. In countries around the world, many people have come to regard literacy rates as important features of the educational, cultural, and economic status of their communities or nations. In some circles these rates are taken to be indicators of national educational success and of economic potential and well-being: the United Nations Development Program, for example, uses three indices in the composition of its "Human Development Index": life expectancy, literacy, and per capita GDP (see Graff, 1987; UNESCO, 1990). One result of the high profile for literacy education is that improving and assessing literacy have been the topics of many debates, and these debates have been not just about the comparative merits of competing theories of reading and writing, or of different ways of teaching them. They are often about "standards," with such standards often referring almost simultaneously to standards of overall educational, cultural, and economic activity. So research and policy development in literacy education have come to enjoy high levels of activity, diversity, and controversy at state, national, and international levels.

Recent literacy education policy initiatives at the national level in Australia have expanded not only the stakes, but also the breadth of the debates, and the kinds of solution and stimulus that enhanced literacy provision is called upon to offer. These debates, and the common practices and aspirations they reflect, make sense only when viewed against the larger changes going on in Australian society. The political, industrial, economic, technological, and cultural patterns that make literacy education "a problem," and that give shape to the solutions that are sought, are themselves

From *The Australian Journal of Language and Literacy*, 23(2), June 2000. Reprinted with permission of the Australian Literacy Educators' Association.

shifting rapidly. Many of these shifts impact directly on what kinds of literacy activities and competencies people value and claim that they or other groups of individuals need.

Of specific interest in this paper is how the debates also need to be viewed as being centrally concerned with what counts as quality literacy teaching, ways of gauging teaching effectiveness, and the nature of assessment itself—its various purposes, and specifically, the problem of unifying assessment and instruction. More than a decade ago, Cole (1988) outlined the problem as follows:

> Assessment is closely associated with two legitimate but different goals— the goal of measurement (and the accountability and policy goals it serves well) and the goal of instruction. The fundamental problem then is the compatibility or incompatibility of these goals. (pp. 108–109)

Although Cole (1988) was referring to the American context, her identification of possible tensions surrounding the different goals for assessment applies equally well to other countries. In the United Kingdom, for instance, the measurement goal has gained considerable influence, as reflected in government plans to close so-called failing or "sink" schools, to introduce performance-related pay, and to continue to publish national test results for Science, Maths, and English in league tables, including at a website.[1] Additionally, there are proposals to attach funding to pupils, not schools, in the name of allowing parents greater choice in school selection, and to get private firms to manage schools under contract to the state.

Currently in Australia there are no such published league tables showing school performance in state-based testing programs. However, the country's first National Plan for literacy and numeracy in schooling, launched in 1998, makes a strong policy commitment to achieving accountability through rigorous testing, measurement, and reporting as early as possible on school entry, and then at Years 3, 5, 7, and 9. (Readers interested in a detailed discussion of the range of state-based testing programs operating throughout Australia are advised to see Wyatt-Smith & Ludwig [1998]). Essentially, the Plan, as elaborated in *Literacy for All: The Challenge for Australian Schooling* (Department of Employment, Education, Training and Youth Affairs, 1998), promotes the understanding that the testing-measurement-reporting mix is the vital means for securing improved literacy and numeracy outcomes. The Plan also sets out the policy testing imperative for

---

1. For interested readers, site details are: http://www.bbc.co.uk/education/schools/. The league table information is one of the options on the home page, the direct link being http://news.bbc.co.uk/hi/english/education/newsid-216000/216975.stm

generating clear, unambiguous information about outcomes, and for providing these to parents and the wider community so that they are informed about school performance, and therefore, school selection. And as the title of the national policy monograph suggests, a distinguishing feature of the Plan is how it reframes the national testing policy initiatives in terms of equity and social justice in schooling, taking up the position that testing is the vital lever for achieving improved outcomes for all.

Against this backdrop, it is timely to ask: how are we balancing the instructional-measurement goals in practice? How do we account for and understand the playing-out of the goals in classrooms, especially in relation to issues of diversity, equity, and inclusive curriculum? Specifically, how do we understand the relationship between state-based standardised literacy testing programs in Years 3, 5, and 7 on the one hand, and on the other, routine classroom assessments, under the control of the teacher? What are the possibilities for congruence between the two? And what is the nature and function of teacher judgement and standards in these different assessment approaches? The remainder of this paper presents the findings of a study that addressed these questions by examining teachers' classroom-based assessment practices and their spoken accounts, recorded in interviews, of being involved with the state-based literacy testing program in Queensland. The sites and participants involved in the study are outlined briefly below.

Sites and participants

Seven teachers from three schools participated in the study. The three schools selected were all part of Education Queensland's *Special Program Schools Scheme*, a Commonwealth-funded, state-administered program designed to measurably improve literacy and numeracy outcomes for educationally disadvantaged students, including students from low socio-economic backgrounds. All three schools catered for students from Years 1 to 7 and had state pre-schools attached. Additionally, all three schools had a high proportion of students whose main language spoken at home was not English. Other noteworthy characteristics of the student population at School 2, identified by the teachers themselves, were the high turnover of students at the school and the high proportion of students with identified learning difficulties. Total enrolments at the three schools and numbers of students whose main language spoken at home is not English are shown in Table 1.

Table 1. School composition (data obtained from the on-line Schools Directory database)

	School 1	School 2	School 3
Total enrolment (February 1998 census)	225	570	218
Number of students whose main language spoken at home is not English	155	139	62
(MLOTE Survey, February 1997)			

At School 1, 127 of the 155 students identify Vietnamese as the main language spoken at home; 8 students give Hindi as the main language spoken at home; 10 other languages are listed, with small numbers of students for each.

At School 2, 82 of the 139 students identify Samoan as the main language spoken at home; 21 students give Vietnamese; smaller numbers speaking other languages (13) are listed.

At School 3, 20 of the 62 students identify Arabic as the main language spoken at home; small numbers speaking other languages (17) are listed.

Characteristics of the seven teacher participants and their distribution across the three schools are shown in Table 2. All the teachers involved in the study were female.

Table 2. Characteristics of teachers

	Year level taught	Years of teaching experience*
School 1		
Teacher 1	Year 3	25 years
Teacher 2	Year 5	30 years
School 2		
Teacher 3	Year 3	15 years
Teacher 4	Year 3	30+ years
Teacher 5	Year 3	15 years
Teacher 6	Year 5	29 years
School 3		
Teacher 7	Year 3	25 years

* Includes time in administrative/advisory roles as well as classroom teaching.

Data collection—nature of data

The nature of the data collected at each site varied in accordance with the number of teachers involved and the nature of their involvement. In general, two main types of classroom data were collected—observation and audio recording of classroom talk, and collection of related classroom artefacts. Classroom talk was transcribed for more detailed analysis.

Additionally, teachers were invited to participate in two semistructured interviews, the first relating to their everyday or routine classroom-based literacy assessment practices and the second, the state-wide literacy testing program in Queensland in the period 1995–1998. The concern was less with the specific design features and tasks that comprise the tests in each of these years than with how the teachers talked about the goals, methods, and consequences of the testing program, and its fit with their own assessment practices. Because of timing issues, not all teachers were able to participate in all parts of the study. Table 3 summarises the distribution of data across the participants. As mentioned earlier, only the findings from the interview data are presented in this paper.

In total, approximately 14 hours of observations were made in Year 3 classrooms while 7 hours of Year 5 classroom observation data were collected.

Table 3. Type and quantity of data obtained at each site

	Year level	Interview data	Classroom observation*
School 1			
Teacher 1	Year 3	Both interviews	3 sessions
Teacher 2	Year 5	Both interviews	2 sessions
School 2			
Teacher 3	Year 3	Both interviews	2 sessions
Teacher 4	Year 3	First interview only	1 session
Teacher 5	Year 3	Both interviews	2 sessions
Teacher 6	Year 5	First interview only	2 sessions
School 3			
Teacher 7	Year 3	Both interviews	No classroom observations

* Although exact start and finish times varied slightly between schools, each school had a morning session from first bell to morning tea (about 2 hours), a middle session from morning tea until lunch (about 1.5 hours), and an afternoon session. No classroom observations were made during the afternoon session.

Analyses of teacher interviews

Each of the teacher interviews was audio-recorded and fully transcribed. The analyses of the interviews focused on what they brought to light about how the teachers saw their classroom-based literacy assessment practices relative to the statewide literacy testing program. Of special interest was how the teachers constructed versions of themselves as teachers and assessors, and versions of the students as learners and participants in the two assessment approaches.

The analyses started from the position that the teachers' accounts of themselves and their students are part of the world they describe (Garfinkel, 1967). As such, readers are asked to consider how the findings presented below relate to other institutional worlds of schooling, literacy education, and its assessment. Further, the analyses drew on the work of Silverman (1993, 1997) who treats interview accounts "as compelling narratives" (p. 114). Specifically, the transcripts were analysed for the attributes, knowledge, and assumptions that the teachers made about themselves, and their students, in the contexts of classroom-based assessment and statewide testing. In this way, the analyses opened up avenues for understanding and practice, in this case with respect to literacy teaching, learning, and assessment. As discussed below, four main issues emerged in the analyses, namely: (1) varying definitions of "essential"; (2) assessment purposes; (3) contexts; and (4) what counts as valued assessment evidence. Each of these issues is addressed separately.

Findings

Policy and teacher accounts of "essential" aspects of literacy

In considering the matter of what counts as essential aspects of literacy and numeracy, two points need to be made at the outset. First, the National Plan gives priority to the measurement of students' progress against agreed benchmarks for Years 3, 5, 7, and 9, and progress towards national reporting on student achievement against these benchmarks (Department of Employment, Education, Training and Youth Affairs, 1998). Second, the national policy defines the benchmark at each year level as intending:

> To set a minimum acceptable standard: a critical level of literacy and numeracy without which a student will have difficulty in making sufficient progress at school. The benchmarks therefore identify the essential aspects of literacy and numeracy. (DEETYA, 1998, p. 23)

According to this statement, the benchmarks capture and make available for scrutiny one account of "essential aspects": an account that is stable and powerful, at least in policy terms, given the stated expectation that it is to be used to inform national reporting on the literacy and numeracy achievement of Australian school-age students.

Given this, it is surprising—even alarming—that the teachers reported that they had no prior knowledge of the National Plan in general or the benchmarks in particular. Further, they did not have a clear sense of the purposes of the Year 3 sampling[2] and Year 5 testing programs, but reported that, as far as they were concerned, the programs had little, if any, curriculum relevance. A Year 5 teacher made the point that the reports "just told you what the children can do and couldn't do on the day, on that particular test." Another teacher commented that the reports "just told me what I knew already." They provided a point-in-time assessment that the teachers saw to be of limited, if any, diagnostic use. They made no mention of using the reported test data to mount intervention programs for individuals or groups of students. A Year 3 teacher talked of her involvement in testing saying:

> When we do the test we're not even going to get the results from the test. So what we'll do with the test is we'll look at it before we send it away. Apparently at the end of the year they're going to send us a follow-up test to see if we've improved. I don't know, but I know that nobody's going to get reports from this. I think they're just getting the standard. I'm not sure. We're just going to do the test, send it away, and we'll never hear another thing. That's how I understand it.

Of interest in this extract is the teacher's use of *we* and *they*. She talked of how "we do the test," and "we're just going to do the test" as though the teachers took themselves to be test takers, along with the students. And in repeating the phrase "we send it away," we hear the teacher emphasising how the test came into the school from an external authority and was returned to that authority, possibly to determine if "we've improved." There is a ring here of the teacher and student pitting themselves against the external examiner, reminiscent of the days of the external junior and senior public examination system. There is also the sense that the teacher was largely "in the dark" about testing and reporting purposes, and did not

---

2. The 1998 Year 5 test was a census test, that is, it was sat by the whole cohort of Year 5 students in the state, with some authorised exemptions. Similarly, the Year 6 test in the preceding three years had been a census test. With the introduction of Year 3 testing in 1998, the policy decision at state level was against census testing and in favour of "sampling," that is, selecting a sample of schools to participate in the testing program for that year.

expect to be informed about what was done with the material "we" exported from the school—"we'll never hear another thing." The comment "nobody's going to get reports from this" shows how, at least from the teacher's viewpoint, the test data were for "in-house" system purposes, with no direct pedagogical implications for her practice.

The point here is that while, officially, the benchmarks identify the essential aspects of literacy, and the design of the Year 5 literacy and numeracy tests are informed by the benchmarks, as well as the state's curriculum, the teachers did not see clear connections among the testing program, official curriculum documents, and locally developed work programs, the National Plan which spawned the benchmarks, the benchmarks, and the reports returned to the school. Certainly they had no knowledge of the benchmarks themselves or what the benchmarks take to be "essential."

What then did the teachers take to be essential in their teaching and assessment practices? While each of the teachers referred to and drew on relevant syllabus documents to construct their own individual accounts of "essential," broadly speaking the accounts tended to fall into two categories. In the first category was talk about "essential" as inevitably defined in terms of the local school and community context and which was understood to be needs-based. As such, what the teachers counted as the essential aspects of literacy and numeracy could vary even widely from year to year, and from student to student, being determined by their perceptions of individual student's needs and capabilities—"where the kids are at and what they can achieve." In accordance with this view, essential was always being redefined and as such, could not be wholly pre-specified. In the second category, there was talk of essential as a core of learning that was currently ill-defined and in need of stabilising through standards specifications. In this category, the teachers talked of the essential aspects as needing to be fixed in the interests of teachers and students.

Category 1: Essential as locally defined

Year 3 teacher:

> No, I don't think what's essential stays the same. Depending on what the class is like, the individuals in the class, I think you're always trying to extend them. So these kids here, I'll be happy if they can understand what they're doing. I'll be happy if they can understand what a maths thing is about and they can understand what they are doing. Like in maths, like Tran, she can do any number fact you give her. You give her 6×9, 12×8, she can answer it. But you ask it to her in the middle of a problem, she doesn't realise she's got to multiply things together. That sort of thing. So with these kids. But I was at, say School B. Those kids are already there.

They do that sort of thing. They come from very literate homes. You know they've got that coming to school, so then you move on to something else, and you try to give them something else. Different areas, different kids, the teachers will be focusing on different things.

In this extract understandings about "essential" hinge on understandings about local school context in the local community: who the students are; their cultural and linguistic backgrounds; their access to resources, both human and material inside and outside the school; and their fluency with spoken, written, and visual English. In effect, what counts as essential is talked about as being inevitably tied to the perceived needs of the cohort, and therefore cannot be wholly pre-specified in authentic or locally relevant ways in syllabus and other policy documents.

Category 2: Essential as core learnings and as standards–related

I think what's essential, it's well, more fixed. I think it needs to be, I mean in a way a standard, you know? I think that there are some variations around the fringe and I've got some students in my class who are, because they may be very advanced in their learning and their use of language, they might, you know, there might be areas that they, like they might be able to spell very difficult scientific words that other students can't spell. On the other hand, I've got students in my class for whom spelling is very difficult so there may be words that they learn to spell that are like a core for them that, you know, almost like a Year 2 level, so within any year level you would have to make provision for students who are either very much up this end or very much down that end. But I still believe that there is a core of essential learning in language.

In this extract, the essential is still associated with responsive, needs-based teaching, a characteristic noted above. Additionally, the essential is framed within the teacher's belief that a core of essential learning in language does exist and that this is tied, albeit in an ill-defined manner, with standards, understood to refer more to content rather than to characteristics or features of achievement levels. Elsewhere in the interview, the teacher reported that in her previous work as an Education Advisor she had encountered repeated calls from teachers asking for greater specificity in terms of pedagogical and assessment content.

Overall, both sets of understandings about "essential" remain fuzzy or undeveloped, with Category 1 tied more tightly to perceptions of students than to understandings about curricular knowledge and skills, and Category 2 presenting a sense of a connection between essential and standards, though the nature of the connection is unclear. When we put the extracts together, what is clear is the need for systems to improve their performance in communicating to teachers information about national and state policy initiatives in literacy testing and how these relate to curriculum and pedagogy. Also clear is the urgent need for teacher involvement in debates about what is essential—essential for what, to whom, and why? This brings us to consideration of assessment purposes and what counts as normal.

Assessment purposes

In the teachers' talk they consistently defined assessment as being primarily for the purpose of capturing the individual student in action across learning situations and tasks. The point of comparison, they said, is the student with his or her self over time. They reported their primary role as being to monitor individual learning in a range of classroom interactions. A Year 3 teacher commented on her assessment purposes and collection methods as follows:

> What I do, I compare the child in relation to where he or she was previously. So to me the only real form of assessing that matters is progress over time, so you know, I have collected samples of a child's writing at the beginning of the year, in the middle and so on, so I'm able to look. We have folders, for every child we have one of these in a filing cabinet...the only assessment that matters is comparison with where they were, so if you look at the beginning of the folder, this is what he was doing in the beginning of Year 1 and if you have a look now it's only two-and-a-half years later, the middle of Year 3 and look at the writing that he's doing...you can really see how much he's learnt, and I think that's fair, I think to compare them with other children, particularly in a school like this. It's not equitable, you know, you've got so many different...such diversity. So it's comparing the child with himself over a period of time. I know that that might not please some people, you know, and I know that there would be people in the community in this school, parents who would want something a little more standardised, more formal, more of a benchmark.

In this extract we hear the teacher's rejection of direct inter-student comparisons in favour of monitoring or tracking individual achievement over time, in fact over years of schooling, including the collection of assessment evidence of a range of types. Assessment, as the teacher talks about it here, is continuous, having a clear curricular and pedagogical relevance, with the insights derived from it used also for reporting purposes. Additionally, there is also a significant hook-up between this type of assessment as active tracking and the teacher's understandings of equity and diversity. She makes clear her position that students come to school as different individuals and that difference has to be factored into how she goes about doing classroom assessment.

The hook-up between assessment and fairness was a common feature of the teachers' talk, with one Year 5 teacher saying:

> Well I don't compare them with other year levels, nor do I compare them with other classes. I only very informally and in my own mind compare them to other children in the class. I don't think that's fair. It just doesn't fit in with the way I think about it. I compare them against themselves and that goes on, you can look at their work, the progression of their work over time. Over the year and it's built up with everything in their work. In their groups if they're performing they can change groups. It's very fluid. I compare them against themselves only really.

Across the corpus of teacher talk there was a strongly voiced commitment to formative assessment, understood as including the dual concerns of diagnosis and improvement, as shown in this extract. The talk demonstrated that teachers could recall, sometimes in vivid detail, how individual students responded to particular activities and resources, and how they could see progress over time. In this monitoring role, the Year 3 teachers referred frequently to the Reading and Writing Continua (Education Department of Western Australia, 1994), indicating its usefulness in informing them about performance characteristics. The Year 5 teachers, however, made no mention of official standards, indicating instead that they relied on their individual histories of evaluative decision-making and internalised or in-the-head standards to determine student progress. This omission reflects how, currently, teachers in Years 4 to 10 do not have available to them authorised, defined standards for use in judging student achievement. One of the implications of this situation seemed to be that while teachers said they were confident about the local appropriateness of their judgements, they reported being uneasy about how these related to teacher judgements of quality in other schools.

The teachers also indicated that they felt uneasy as they anticipated how successive groups of their students would manage test demands. The test situation was far from routine and students had to be readied, even rehearsed, for taking the test. The teachers' talk indicated a sense of vulnerability, even nervousness, as they worried about how their curriculum planning equipped students with the knowledge and skills necessary to satisfy test demands. The test represented the unknown, and as mentioned above, its purpose remained unclear for teacher and student alike. In effect, it was something imposed from above. For some of the teachers, it raised to the fore the issue of what represents *normal*, saying,

I'm worried that the people who do this test have a different idea of what is a normal Grade 5 than what I do. Well I mean everybody would be worried about that.

The issue of normalcy seemed to have less to do with demonstrated ability level than with cultural capital. Did the students have the cultural knowledge necessary to answer the questions? A Year 3 teacher reflected on this as follows:

> When it comes to this [testing] I panicked. I thought, oh no, what if they're going to be asked to do something that is in the syllabus, but we haven't written down for [suburb X] children. So then we went through yesterday and looked at the things that they could be asked to do. And so I'm sort of going over it now with them in case it turns up next week in the test. So they're not going to panic and say "I've never seen this before. I can't do it." I mean I don't expect it to be that difficult. I expect that the test will say, you know, give a recount of something. Well they can do recounts with their eyes closed. We do it all the time. But it is a bit of a worry that they'll be asked to do something that [suburb X] children have not been taught how to do just because, maybe it's in the syllabus and we're planning on doing it in maybe Grade 4 or Grade 5 and other schools might have done it in Grade 3.

The contribution of cultural capital to test performance came home forcibly to me last week again, when a Year 5 teacher reported that the 1999 literacy test required students to answer questions about a reproduced Internet page. He said that the one and only computer in his classroom was not connected to the Net and most of his students did not have Net access in their homes. On the test day, he reported that many students looked puzzled when they saw the Internet page and asked him to explain it. His reply—"This is a test. Just see what sense you make of it by yourself." This example calls into question the particular criteria that had been chosen and applied to this year's literacy test in Queensland: how was it scrutinised for curriculum relevance and equity considerations? It also raises the issue of what is actually being assessed, given the teacher's comment that the Internet text set for assessing reading was unfamiliar to many of his students. Additionally, while it is widely recognised that technological literacy is a vital concern in literacy education, we need to query whether a paper and pencil test with a static print text is the best means for assessing such literacy. Attention now turns to consider how the teachers talked about "context" in classroom assessment and testing situations.

The significance of context(s)

The term "context" frequently recurred in teachers' talk about classroom assessment practices and testing programs. More specifically, their use of the term *context* was tied to understandings about teacher—student relationships and the ways in which those relationships are shaped by various conceptualisations of context. Of specific interest are, first, the concept of context as it applies to developing in students a sense of the authentic or real-life purpose(s) of activities; second, teachers' understanding about students' out-of-school contexts; and third, the context of the statewide test. Each of these will be considered separately.

Teaching context

The teachers talked of devoting considerable time and energy to "building pedagogical context" in order to establish learning as purposeful. They talked of how purposeful learning hinged on students having an authentic cultural and social context for the activities they were required to undertake at school. Essentially, building context was, they said, foundational to good practice. One teacher spoke of this as it applies to teaching writing as follows:

> You know, that's the important thing, that when you ask them to write something you have to first of all create the context, you have to create a purpose for the writing, you have to create a sense of audience, you know, who they're writing for and so on. If all that's done well and you've done a lot of work in terms of preparing them for that, then they often write quite well. And with regard to spelling, again it depends on what, what the context that we've been using, you know, they might be able to spell "Nintendo," but not spell "crown," you know, for example, because they're words that they're using more than others.

In this conversation we hear about the teacher's understanding of writing pedagogy as being "first of all" to "create the context." We also hear how the teacher deliberately connects context with purpose and audience in her classroom practice in order to prepare students for writing, including spelling. She also indicates that this preliminary work has benefit—"they often write quite well."

Students' life contexts

The teachers' talk also brought to light their keen interest in connecting teaching, learning, and assessment activities with the students' outside-of-school experiences as a way of achieving relevance. Taking account of context then, was a matter of looking outside the school window and knowing about student characteristics relating to geographical location and cultural and linguistic backgrounds—their life contexts. According to the teachers, the authenticity and usefulness of assessment evidence generated in the classroom depended on the knowledge they developed of students' life contexts as well as the teachers' ability and willingness to design activities that were responsive to those contexts. A Year 5 teacher spoke of the need for responsive practice as follows:

> Because students learn language in context...and I believe that's the way to teach language as well is to create some kind of social context. That social context is determined very much by the cultural context in which the children are, so the children in, let's say you know, Camooweal or the children in an Aboriginal community in North Queensland, for example, have a very different cultural context from the children who are living in let's say the Gold Coast or suburban Brisbane, you know, or different again from children who are living in the country, so the problem with the essential elements is how do you define those and at the same time take into account the different cultural social contexts in which children are learning language, and that's why the new syllabus has not done that. It says that the context is derived from the children's everyday living and school subject matter, so you can teach information reports in Grade 3, but whether you choose to teach them about the salt water crocodile or birds or spiders is determined by where you're living and what's around you.

In this extract we hear the teacher bringing into focus the need, in this case, for language activities to be anchored into cultural and social contexts, as well as the need for the teacher to relate classroom practice to "children's everyday living." We also hear the teacher's understanding that the present Queensland *English Syllabus for Years 1 to 10* (1994) authorises teachers to take account of outside-of-school contexts or what she refers to as "the different cultural social contexts in which children are learning language."

The required shift in teacher–student relationship

In both of the above notions of context, there is a clear emphasis on the teacher and student in a partnership: the teacher is the master who deliberately and carefully scaffolds learning for the student apprentice, thereby inducting her into cultural knowledges. Further, we hear of how the teaching-learning relationship is foundational to how assessment happens in the classroom. In short, there is no clear demarcation between teaching and learning on the one hand, and on the other, assessment. On the designated test program days, however, at least for a few hours, sitting the test required a radical shift in the teacher–student relationship. For the teacher at least, there was the understanding that on test day, the paper was to be completed as far as possible in silence and as a solo performance. In the test situation, the teacher understood that she was to be detached—to keep an observable distance from student performance.

Teachers were well aware that the students needed to be readied for the test situation and, more importantly, for the inevitable change in teacher–student relationship that this brought with it. In the following extract, a Year 3 teacher talks of her work in preparing students for the test and relationship change.

> So we'll go through all the talk with it and getting them ready and discussing the topic and looking for words and things like that. And then I told them I can't put it all up on the board for them. I can't plan it. Because that's the sort of thing we do, and they write from the board. So, what I'm trying to do is to get them to do that for themselves. So, you know, we put up these boxes and I say now you tell me the words, now you write it down. I'm trying to get them to do it themselves but they're not used to it.

The final sentence "I'm trying to get them to do it themselves but they're not used to it" suggests the teacher's sense of how the context of the test fundamentally alters how teacher and student "do" school writing. And in the following extract, we hear a teacher who talks of how the routine teacher–student relationship has to change, given that the testing purpose is point-in-time measurement.

> If you're just getting students, if you're just setting them a little writing task and saying OK, go and write it, then you're not going to be doing all that scaffolding. But that's a control situation, that's a test situation, isn't it? I mean, if your aim is to have some kind of national benchmark, and you've got to provide the same conditions, then you either, I mean how do you say "Teachers you can do this much scaffolding and not this much," you know? Either they do none, but you know, scaffolding is part of the teaching. This is not a teaching, this is a testing thing, so you live with that.

The teacher's distinction in the final sentence—"This is not a teaching, this is a testing thing"—is vital in coming to understand the current relationship between classroom assessments and the testing program. Essentially, it comes down to the distinction between formative and summative assessment, where teachers saw their assessment practices as primarily formative in nature, being concerned with diagnosis and improvement, rather than with grading or the awarding of summative grades. The teachers talked of themselves as key participants, with students, in their classroom-based assessments, designing and teaching the assessment activities, working with students to enable them to complete the activities successfully.

What counts as valued assessment evidence?

The fact is that the teachers are well placed to make direct first-hand observations of and judgements about student achievement. They are well placed to provide valid assessment evidence in the form of portfolios containing evidence collected over time. However, they report a lack of confidence in the reliability of those judgements. The following extract shows how their uncertainty can be traced directly to at least two main sources.

> Do I have a clear picture of student achievement? Probably not, no, I'd have to say I really, I don't feel as if I really have got a really good grasp. I mean I have got gut feelings, because you know, I know my students very well and I believe I know what they can and can't do, but I guess it's a little bit of that feeling of that unless it's objective and unless it's formalised, you know, a real formal collection of data, you don't really trust it. If I go to do something that's an assessment activity, often it will turn into, because I scaffold a lot, because I say well, you know, because I can see that there are students having problems with it, I can't let them just sit there feeling as if they can't do something and failing, so therefore I intervene and they come up to me and they say "I can't do this" and I say "All right, who else is having trouble? Come over here and we'll do it together," and before I know it I've taught it, so I don't have ways...I mean I have ways, but often the opportunities that I have, the opportunities that I create from collecting hard data on the students' abilities, I lose it because I've scaffolded too much, I've started teaching and before I know it I don't really know whether they can do it or not.
>
> I mean I know, for example, that they don't know this stuff or they can't do it, so it's really I guess my teacher judgement that is probably more accurate in that sense, and I guess that's where sometimes as teachers we don't trust that or we forget to formalise, we forget to write that down, you know.

In this extract, we hear the teacher talking about the competing demands she faces as she juggles different assessment purposes. While she may set out to generate what she refers to as hard data, initially wanting to stay removed from the assessment to see what students can do, alone and unaided, it seems the students actively call her in to participate in the assessment activity. What emerges is a clear picture of the students working to maintain the teaching-learning-assessment connection in routine classroom practice, even on those occasions when the teacher planned to generate hard data for measurement purposes. Also in this extract, we hear of the teacher's need for clearly defined assessment standards. It is hardly surprising that teachers report a lack of confidence in their judgements when, currently, they do not have access to explicitly defined year level standards to scrutinise and defend those judgements. Until such standards are developed and implemented, and teacher judgement is targeted as a professional development priority, the danger is that the statewide testing programs and the results that they generate may be viewed as having an authority greater than that attributed to teachers' classroom assessments, even by the teachers themselves. Already there are observable, mounting fears about the use of test results as reliable evidence of teacher effectiveness. One teacher revealed her fears as follows:

> Probably what worries me most is that if the results are low or the benchmarks are not met by a certain school, is it then considered that that school (1) is no good, and (2) the teachers at the school are no good? I think that's really hard and there's teachers who work in schools where there are quite a few difficulties for children with reading and writing and numeracy. Well where do we stand, you know? I think you're going to get other schools where the parents are supporting them—we don't get any of that here.... You feel like you're hitting your head against a brick wall. And the other thing here that we find difficult is that we have such a transient population as well, so you think you're going along nicely and then the next minute the whole class changes, or half your class changes. So you just start all over again and there are your percentages dropping down, and that's no reflection on the school or the teachers. That's my big concern, it really is. Testing and benchmarks have got to be handled carefully and this thing that was in the paper about, you know, being divulged to the public. OK, if all the facts are added to it, but you know, why? Because, I mean I could sit there and say oh, wasn't I the best teacher last year, look at all my Grade 3s. Then the year before I'd be going, I'd be the worst teacher in the school because I had all these low kids. I mean, you can really get yourself your self-esteem knocked at a place like here, I think.

This extract shows the teacher's attempt at exoneration—the school is exonerated in the talk from major responsibility for low literacy achievement—and the allocation of blame. We hear the blame focused on student deficits, parental involvement, and transfers—all factors over which teachers have no control and yet they remain, according to the teachers, powerful influences on learning outcomes. There is also a clear voicing of vulnerability—"you can really get yourself, your self-esteem knocked at a place like here"—accompanied by a fear of being classified publicly as a failing school/failing teacher.

Outlining the challenges in the search for congruence in assessment

Implicit in much of the preceding analysis is the need to improve ways of assessing literacy, both in classroom-based assessments and in large-scale, standardised testing programs. This section outlines five main challenges that we need to address if we are to achieve congruence in our ways of assessing literacy in schooling.

First and foremost, the education community needs to be clear about the purposes of various assessment programs, and how the various programs relate in terms of purpose, one to the other. If statewide testing programs are to have a genuine purpose of *improving* outcomes, as distinct from *reporting* outcomes, then we need to reach agreement that the teacher, not the test, is the primary change agent. If we agree on this, then we must bring teacher judgement to centre stage. The point is that teacher judgement is central to a much-needed review and discussion of all performance evidence, including that generated in standardised testing and in classroom-based programs. The challenge is to confirm the consonance of the evidence or to identify outlying aspects of the students' performances. In short, teacher judgement can be used effectively to interrogate the links between the school assessment program and the evidence it generates and the evidence generated in the test program.

Essentially, we need to map the nature and scope of the evidence generated in the standardised testing program, and the nature and scope of the evidence generated in classroom-based assessment programs. We need to know how the two interface, and what they tell us, separately and together, so that we know the whole assessment story. What is the nature of the knowledge and skills assessed in the two programs? And what definitions of literacy and numeracy are informing the programs? If we keep the programs separate at policy level, we run the risk of going down the pathway leading to test results being used to announce so-called beacon and failing schools.

Second, we need to re-value teacher judgement, on the understanding that it lies "at the heart of good teaching and good assessment" (Sadler, 1986, p. 6). Currently however, there is an urgent need to invest in teacher judgement, training it up through professional development programs focusing sharply on assessment, and through system support mechanisms including those provided through internal and external moderation networks. The extracts considered earlier show how teachers face competing demands as they struggle to distinguish formative and summative assessment purposes. Teacher professional development programs are needed to assist teachers to distinguish between assessment with teaching–learning significance and assessment with measurement significance, showing how they are best placed to do both in their classroom practice.

Third, there is an urgent need to make explicit performance expectations for literacy education: what is it that we expect students to be able to know and do? There is an urgent need for anchoring teacher judgement into standards, written as verbal descriptors of outcomes with accompanying exemplars that make clear how each exemplar matches the characteristics of the stated standard. Currently, while teachers in the early years can look to the *Continua* for some standards advice, teachers in Years 5 to 10 make judgements about student literacy and numeracy in the absence of a clearly defined standards framework.

Fourth, we need to use the testing programs themselves as a professional development opportunity. This can be achieved by feeding back to schools not only quantitative reports, but also reports about the features of good assessment task design at various year levels. Also, we need to make available for teachers information about the scoring guides applied to student scripts in the testing programs and the training given to the assessors.

Finally, we need to be mindful that all assessment activities are contextualised and value-laden. There is no such thing as value-free assessment! The setting of cut scores in national equating exercises is included here. Dwyer (1998) made this point, writing that "any use of a cut point, no matter how sophisticated or elaborate its technical apparatus, is at heart a values decision. The underlying question in setting any cut score can be phrased quite simply: 'How much is enough?' There is, of course, no technical answer to that question; there is always a value answer to it" (p. 18). So, in informing the much-needed debate about how assessment can be retheorised to take account of diversity, we should know more about how test scores are actually treated with respect to cut scores and who takes the responsibility for and acts on these decisions in institutional uses.

In conclusion, I am mindful of the divergent priorities and goals of key education stakeholders in Australia, and aware of the pressure on some to follow short-term political imperatives of appearing to be delivering improved results. The challenge for the educational community is to ward off this pressure, focusing instead on providing support for the long-term professional development change necessary to effect actual pedagogical change and improved outcomes. If the aim of standardised testing, measurement, and reporting, as proposed in the National Plan, is to secure literacy for all Australians, then teachers must be key players in instigating, developing, implementing, and reviewing systems of assessment reform. As all teachers know only too well, assessment procedures, of themselves, do not necessarily lead to improvement.

Acknowledgments

I wish to acknowledge the helpful feedback and assistance provided by Ms. Jill Ryan and Ms. Stephanie Gunn in the preparation of this paper.

REFERENCES

Cole, N.S. (1988). A realist's appraisal for unifying instruction and assessment. In C.V. Bunderston (Ed.), *Assessment in the service of learning*. Princeton, NJ: Educational Testing Service.

Department of Education, Qld. (1994). *English syllabus for Years 1 to 10*. Brisbane: Author.

Department of Employment, Education, Training and Youth Affairs. (1998). *Literacy for all: The challenge for Australian schools* (Australian Schooling Monograph Series No. 1, AGPS). Canberra: Author.

Dwyer, C.A. (1998). Testing and affirmative action: Reflections in a time of turmoil. *Educational Researcher, 27*(9), 17–18.

Education Department of Western Australia. (1994). *First Steps: Reading: Developmental continuum*. Melbourne: Longman.

Education Department of Western Australia. (1994). *First Steps: Writing: Developmental continuum*. Melbourne: Longman

Garfinkel, J. (1967). *Studies in ethnomethodology*. Englewood Cliffs, NJ: Prentice Hall.

Graff, H.J. (1987). *The labyrinths of literacy: Reflections on past and present*. Sussex, UK: Falmer Press.

Sadler, D.R. (1986). Subjectivity, objectivity, and teachers' qualitative judgments. *Assessment Unit Discussion Paper 5*. Brisbane: Board of Secondary School Studies.

Silverman, D. (1993). *Interpreting qualitative data. Methods for analysing talk, text and interaction*. London: Sage.

Silverman, D. (Ed.). (1997). *Qualitative research. Theory, method and practice*. London: Sage.

UNESCO. (1990). *Basic education and literacy: World statistical indicators*. Paris: Author.

Wyatt-Smith, C.M., & Ludwig, C. (1998). Teacher roles in large scale literacy assessment. *Curriculum Perspectives, 18*(3), 1–14.

Reading literacy test data: Benchmarking success?

Nola Alloway and Pam Gilbert

On 15 September 1997, the (then) Minister for Schools, Vocational Education and Training, the Hon. Dr. David Kemp MP, released results of the National School English Literacy Survey with a special report, *Literacy Standards in Australia*. The results were, Dr. Kemp claimed, "a national disgrace," and, not surprisingly, crisis rhetoric was subsequently used in the popular media to denounce education systems, schools, and parents for what was claimed to be a decline in national literacy standards of Year 3 and Year 5 children across the country.

The national survey has been criticised on a number of accounts, including its determination of "cut-off scores," its location of literacy benchmarks, and the construction of literacy implicitly endorsed. Notwithstanding this, however, results from such surveys have been widely used as evidence that "a problem" exists with literacy: a problem with how literacy is taught; a problem with literacy practices in homes and communities; and a problem with the lack of literacy skills that students from some cultural backgrounds bring with them to schools.

Less widely cited, however, are concerns about how national literacy testing is indicative of the competitive, individualistic discourses of contemporary political times; how it contributes to perpetuating pathological stereotypes about groups of children and their families; or how it clings to a concept of literacy which ignores the changing face of language practices in the workplace and in society. Poor literacy test results come to be equated with national economic and social decline and the breakdown of what could be identified as an historic—Anglo-Saxon—cultural hegemony, rather than with any valuable measure of young people's competence with the literacies of their homes and communities.

In this article we will look more carefully at the "problems" with literacy, and we do so from a background of concern for the democratic processes of schooling. Both of us have a long history of working on issues

From *The Australian Journal of Language and Literacy*, 21(3), October 1998. Reprinted with permission of the Australian Literacy Educators' Association. A version of this article was first presented as a keynote address at the New South Wales Literacy Strategies Briefing Day, Sydney, 16 February 1998.

of gender, disadvantage, and schooling practices, and most recently we have worked on several "boys and literacy" projects. This work has highlighted for us the misleading nature of crisis rhetoric about literacy test results, but it has also made us recognise the potential of using aspects of such test results for a reformist agenda. A national testing agenda is not one of our choosing, and would not be our preferred model of assessing students' literacy competence. However the data that such testing consistently produces make a strong case for asking of education why it is that some groups of children repeatedly do less well than others on standardised measures of literacy.

We will initially offer here readings of a range of literacy test data, before moving from that to a consideration of how we might use such data to recognise effective literacy practice. Our article will be grounded in our experience with the boys and literacy issue, because we have found it to be a good example of the tightrope walk that literacy educators must practice (see Alloway & Gilbert, 1997).

Reading literacy test data

In 1996 the Australian Council for Educational Research (ACER) was commissioned by the federal government to collect data related to literacy achievement at school. With a focus on achievement levels in the early years, ACER randomly selected for testing 8,200 Year 3 and Year 5 students from across state borders. ACER's brief was to establish national base-line data on literacy achievement and to set reading and writing achievement data against benchmarks of literacy success for these age/Year levels. Literacy benchmarks are meant to represent minimum acceptable standards, without which a student will have difficulty making sufficient progress at school.

It is worth noting that in the benchmarking exercise reported in *Literacy Standards in Australia* (Masters, 1997), and in subsequent media accounts, the term "literacy" achievement is used loosely in that the report refers only to reading and writing performance benchmarks—despite the fact that the mapping exercise completed by ACER included data on reading, writing, speaking, listening, and viewing. Most teachers would be familiar with a definition of literacy which encompassed a broad range of literate practices, including forms that the newer electronic cultures have spawned. As many literacy educators would now argue, and as the fourth issue in 1996 of the *Australian Journal of Language and Literacy* demonstrated, the impact of literacy practices that have moved from page to screen, and the particular competencies such shifts require, are crucial for schools to engage with.

However it is reading and writing that is the focus for the ACER material, and some of the key findings are as follows:

Performance in reading

- 73% of Year 3 students met the Year 3 standard
- 27% of Year 3 students did not meet the Year 3 standard

- 71% of Year 5 students met the Year 5 standard
- 29% of Year 5 students did not meet the Year 5 standard

Performance in writing

- 72% of Year 3 students met the Year 3 standard
- 28% of Year 3 students did not meet the Year 3 standard

- 67% of Year 5 students met the Year 5 standard
- 33% of Year 5 students did not meet the Year 5 standard

Turning the gaze on early childhood

As with any results that are used to "worry" the nation, the bureaucratic gaze inevitably turns on those who have responsibility for children's earliest experiences. And so, the critical gaze is now more often turned to the early years of schooling to determine how it is that so many young children can fail to reach the national benchmarks for reading and writing, benchmarks that presumably predict the ease or difficulty students will experience in successfully negotiating the school curriculum. As argued in the report on *Literacy Standards in Australia*:

> Students' foundational skills in reading and writing are established during the early years of school. Mastery of fundamental reading and writing skills by the end of Year 3 is essential if students are to make adequate progress during their primary years. The extension of these fundamental skills by the end of primary school is essential if students are to be successful learners across the curriculum in secondary schools and beyond. (Masters, 1997, p. 2)

It is unlikely that early childhood educators will argue about the value and significance of children's early experiences with literacy. Few are likely to dispute that it is in children's interests to have mastered fundamental reading and writing skills before venturing into middle school. However, the data are more complex than might first appear.

The National English Literacy Survey, for instance, offers a closer look at exactly who is falling below the benchmarks. As reflected in the results, identifiable groups of children fail to make the grade as measured against the reading and writing performance standards. As the report (Masters, 1997) notes, some groups of students perform far less well than do others.

- Boys as a group achieved significantly lower scores than girls as a group, in both reading and writing, at both Year 3 and Year 5 levels.
- Against both reading and writing benchmarks, children from low socio-economic backgrounds scored lower than those from medium socio-economic backgrounds who in turn scored lower than those from high socio-economic backgrounds. The gap between these sub-groups increased from Year 3 to Year 5.
- Children from language backgrounds other than English met the benchmark standards for reading and writing less often than those from English language backgrounds.
- A very low percentage of children identified within a special Indigenous sample met benchmark standards for reading and writing in Year 3 and Year 5.

While it is gender that clearly remains a key predictor of literacy achievement, groups of students with least access to social privilege and economic resources continue to score in the lower ranges of literacy results. For example, consider data from the survey in Table 1 about reading standards at Year 5 (Masters, 1997, p. 15).

The social inequality of these test results seems to be one of the most significant features of the ACER data. How is it that such unequal social access to school literacy practices continues in the late twentieth century?

Table 1. Reading standards at Year 5

Year 5 Reading	Percentage meeting the standard	Percentage not meeting the standard
Main sample (total)	71	29
Males	65	35
Females	76	24
Language background other than English	56	44
English language background	72	28
High socio-economic status	87	13
Medium socio-economic status	71	29
Low socio-economic status	47	53
Special Indigenous sample	23	77

Yet how do we account for gender as a key predictor here? Boys, as a whole group, are not socially disadvantaged, but at every turn boys do less well on literacy tests than do girls who have similar socio-economic and cultural resources. How does gender, particularly masculinity, impact upon the form of literacy achievement measured in mapping exercises like the English National Literacy Survey? And what might this tell us about the construction of literacy in the late twentieth century?

Turning the gaze away from the individual child

Perhaps the most insidious danger for literacy educators is to assume that literacy "problems" are essentially "individual" problems, and the competitive, individualistic discourses of standardised testing reinforce this reading of the data. Steeped in time-honoured philosophies of individual growth and development, early childhood and primary school educators understandably will be tempted to begin their investigation of low level literacy achievement at the point of the individual child's accomplishments. There is a seductive ease in assuming that poor literacy outcomes reflect the individual pathology of poor performers. Nevertheless, as the ACER report makes clear, there is bountiful evidence to suggest that the picture is conceptually far more complex.

And the ACER material is supported by other literacy data. Four Australian state education departments, for instance, have released gender-based analyses of senior secondary results for subject English. In each state—Western Australia, Queensland, South Australia, and New South Wales—girls significantly outperformed boys in terms of school-based literacy achievement. And, it seems, this pattern of boys' lower level literacy-related performance is already apparent in earlier years. An analysis of results of the New South Wales Year 3 Basic Skills Test for literacy shows girls as a group outperforming boys as a group (Davy, 1995).

Interestingly, as well as documenting the average difference between girls and boys, the New South Wales data track the interplay between gender and socio-economic ranking. Socio-economic background clearly impacted on test outcomes. For instance, boys with the highest socio-economic rankings achieved higher scores than girls with the lowest socio-economic rankings, and, tellingly, boys in the lowest socio-economic groupings scored worse than any other group. Clearly, regardless of the social and economic resources available to them through their families, gender remained a significant predictor of success on these tests. At each socio-economic ranking, boys scored less well than their sisters who shared their level of social and economic privilege.

Extending the argument further, Yunupingu (1994) reports that Aboriginal and Torres Strait Islander students generally achieve lower literacy scores in early schooling than other Australian students. While Aboriginal and Torres Strait Islander students in urban areas fare better than those in rural and remote areas, the report notes that "gender patterns are similar to those found for all Australian primary school students" whereby "Aboriginal and Torres Strait Islander girls consistently record higher achievements in literacy than boys.." (Yunupingu, p. 24).

Literacy, remediation, and masculinity

The history of dealing with those at school who under-perform in literacy has traditionally focused on skills-based remediation of individual children. It is assumed that those who do not perform well have a learning deficit, either intellectual or social, that leads consequentially to remediation. The "intellectual deficit" condition assumes that, unlike those children who succeed, those marked for remediation simply fail to grasp critical content from the teacher's expert delivery of knowledge. The fault in this instance lies within the intellectual competence of the individual child. By contrast, the "social deficit" condition implies that the child's family background is the root of failure. That is, the particular child does not have the social resources to be truly "ready" for the experiences of schooling.

Whichever the deficit, the remedy is located in the individual child's remediation to make him/her fit the expectations and processes of schooling. In these ways, the processes of schooling that enfranchise particular groups while disenfranchising others escape interrogation and are understood to be innocuous, impartial, and beyond suspicion. The impetus is to reform the child rather than the curriculum, since the source of the trouble is seen to lie outside of the parameters of "schooling as usual."

There is no question that in some instances individual remediation may be the appropriate course of action. However, when identifiable groups rather than random selections of children present as underachievers, as "at risk" students, and as school failures, then remediation may not be the preferred response. Experiences with expensive remedial reading programs and reading intervention schemes, for example, have obviously not had the desired effect on boys, who form the bulk of participants in such programs. Something else is involved here, which cannot easily be explained by individualistic or remediation discourses.

We would argue that the first level of questioning about literacy test failure should logically revolve around why particular groups perform at consistently lower levels than others. Why do boys as a group perform less well than girls in literacy-related tasks? Why do boys with the lowest socio-economic rankings perform least well of any group? How is it that boys with the highest socio-economic rankings perform at lower levels than girls from the same group, but at higher levels than girls who live in families where fewer social and economic resources are available to them?

However, we would argue that an equally important level of questioning must address the constructions of literacy tested and valued within school, system, and national literacy agendas. What does the unequal performance of students—as groups—suggest to us about the forms of literacy valued and endorsed?

Moving to a different framework

A team of researchers at James Cook University has proposed a different framework for looking at literacy performance. The approach we adopt in *Boys and Literacy: Professional Development Units* (Alloway & Gilbert, 1997) moves away from focusing on what is wrong with individual children, to avoid the trap of automatically pathologising children and their families. Rather, we look at how boys are positioned within social and pedagogical practices that make their lesser performance in literacy-related tasks understandable and predictable, and at how literacy, as a school practice, privileges particular forms of social knowledge that may well seem irrelevant, and undesirable, for some groups of boys.

Concerns about boys' literacy performance usually refer specifically to their demonstrated competence in the context of literacy as it is done and evaluated in schools, despite the fact that this represents only one literacy site, and one broad set of literacy practices. Many boys have literacy skills that are not recognised in the classroom, but that are potentially powerful and useful in the communication technologies of the future, and these technological skills are often developed in the early years for boys (see Alloway, 1995). However the forms of literate competence required for surfing the Net, reading video screens, and engaging with computers do not figure highly in school measurements of literacy.

An important point to remember, therefore, is that boys may underachieve in school-based literacy, but they do not necessarily underachieve in other forms of socially valued, and more "desirable," literate practice. In fact, we may well want to ask why it is that the new literate subject of the postmodern world, who lives and plays with and through the multimedia representations of globalised culture and the new "literacies" such a culture creates, is not more prominently represented in school cultures and school pedagogies.

The changing "literate" self

Literacy as it is done in the early grades of school revolves somewhat fluidly around learning to read and to write in clearly defined ways, using authorised texts and teaching practices. As children move through grade levels, they move through regimes of texts and practices: reading kits and activities, spelling and handwriting skills, comprehension tests, vocabulary exercises, essay writing, oral and dramatic performance, sustained silent reading, and aesthetic response to literary texts. What these early schooling practices have in common is that they require students to demonstrate a willingness to be regulated—both physically and emotionally—in specific ways: to sit still, to be silent, to work with utensils in defined and authorised ways, to respond in appropriate ways (Luke, 1992).

Here boys have to learn how to produce "good work": to be tidy and neat by using writing implements correctly; to be careful and custodial with texts by holding and managing books properly; to be socially compliant, by performing literacy practices like morning talk presentations, class and group discussions, and chats with the teacher. Angela Phillips, for instance, suggests that "good work" at primary school is "just like being good for Mummy...": that it does nothing to enhance "a child's sense of masculinity" (Phillips, 1993, p. 231). While all schooling requires degrees of physical and emotional regulation, this seems to be particularly the case in the literacy classroom.

So what's this got to do with gender and with boys' school-based literacy achievement? Because so much time in the early years of school is devoted to learning to read and to write, and to learning the discourse patterns of school talk and discipline, it must be easy for boys to see "reading" and "school" as almost synonymous, and for literacy and schooling discourses to become closely intertwined. Being good at literacy comes to mean being good at school: schooling and literacy coalesce. Or, as primary school boys interviewed for a Queensland study said:

...boys who are good at school are the ones who like books....

They're into work. Wear proper uniform. Always neat. Never late for school. Boys who are good at school like being by themselves and sitting down and reading and stuff. (Gilbert & Gilbert, in press)

Martino's (1995) interviews with secondary school boys demonstrate similar responses, and Martino suggests that homophobia, and a general fear of being identified as non-masculine, may feature in regulating boys' engagement with English. One of the secondary school boys he interviewed claimed that:

English is more suited to girls because it's not the way guys think...this subject is the biggest load of bullshit I have ever done. Therefore, I don't particularly like this subject. I hope you aren't offended by this, but most guys who like English are faggots. (Martino, 1995, p. 354)

However, boys do not suddenly begin resisting school-based literacy tasks in secondary classrooms; the process of alienation is identifiable in the early years of compulsory schooling (see Orlandi, 1996). In Orlandi's Grade 1–2 composite class, for instance, boys produced approximately half of what girls produced in terms of written text. Boys were able to resist writing stories by "thinking" until writing time was over. While Martino's secondary boys were able to articulate their rejection of the literacy classroom in terms of masculine and sexual identity, Orlandi's Grade 1 and 2 boys naively complained that writing stories was "dumb" and "stupid." More generally, it seems that boys write less, read less, and engage with domains of subject matter that are not usually endorsed by the school (see Gilbert, 1994; Poynton, 1985).

Learning how to "do" school thus becomes very much about learning the appropriate patterns of talk, of listening, of writing, and of reading for the school context. This means learning how to perform school and how to insert the body not only into the gendered, social landscape of the school, but also into the regulation and surveillance of what becomes the "feminised" literacy classroom. Whereas much of a girl's social learning has introduced her to performances of submission, passivity, and courtesy, much of a boy's learning has been different. His experiences through sport and leisure have introduced him to performances of activity and larrikin individualism, and to masculinities that are embodied in competitive, aggressive, and homophobic ways.

This can be particularly at odds with school practices that have come to be associated with literature and response to literature. For example, many of the most familiar school literacy practices require that students accomplish the processes of self-disclosure, introspection, empathic response, and personalised and creative expression (Gilbert, 1989; Hunter, 1988; Patterson, 1997). The literate student within these discourses, for example, is able to lay bare the soul: to engage in literacy practices that describe feelings and emotions, and which locate the writer/reader as a sensitive and aesthetic subject who derives pleasure from print and the literary experience. Even in the early years of schooling, the focus in the literacy classroom is often on personalised expression and response to teacher-sanctioned texts.

Constructing a masculine self

Meanwhile, outside the context of the school, boys are encouraged to understand themselves very differently. As opposed to the social construction of literacy as feminised practice, boys are expected to understand themselves within sets of masculinised practice. Their subjectivity is to be marked as different from, and oppositional to, that which is associated with the feminine. Hegemonic masculinity is not done in terms of self-disclosure, introspection, personalised and creative expression, but rather in terms of an outside-of-self, objectified expression. A focus on the psyche, on analysis of self and others, on personal relations, on moral regulation, is not endorsed within hegemonic standards of masculinity. Outward-looking, masculinity prefers to concentrate on things outside of self, rather than on the self.

While boys are required to comply with the school's construction of the regulated literate student, the social construction of hegemonic masculinity promotes masculine subjectivity as less regulated, less conforming, and less compliant than schooling practices accommodate. Hegemonic masculinity ultimately refuses to be regulated or controlled. Affiliation with hegemonic standards of masculinity advances an identity that is more maverick, self-styled, and independent than can be expressed within the processes of school regulation.

Constructions of literacy and masculinity open out a field of play where abrasive interactions are inevitable. Some groups of boys may find the press to become insiders to the literacy experience particularly threatening to their masculinity. Issues of class, ethnicity, race, and sexuality may be crucial in determining how boys resolve tensions involved in maintaining masculine identity while simultaneously responding to institutional requirements to take themselves up as literate school subjects (Gilbert & Gilbert, in press). Some boys may reject the requirement to engage in the "feminised practices" of the literacy classroom as the friction with their masculinity is too keenly experienced.

The differences between groups of boys in their response to literacy tasks need, however, to be carefully monitored. The complex relationships between class, ethnicity, and masculinity, for instance, may mean that privileged groups of boys are more likely to be encouraged to accept forms of school regulation in anticipation of career and professional rewards in the post-schooling period. The willingness to take up positions as "literate" subjects will consequently be dependent upon a range of factors associated with ethnicity, with class, with sexuality, and with the versions of masculinity boys find desirable.

Concluding remarks

Developmental continua and individual performance indicators cannot help us to understand why, for example, Aboriginal and Torres Strait Islander students living in urban areas achieve higher literacy scores than those living in remote and rural areas; why boys generally score less well than girls; why boys from high socio-economic backgrounds outperform girls from low socio-economic backgrounds; or why boys with the lowest socio-economic rankings—along with Indigenous boys—score worst of all. Pedagogies and intervention strategies that centre on individual profiling may, perhaps, be helpful in monitoring some aspects of literacy competence, but they are inadequate in understanding the complexity of literacy performance and achievement.

Teachers need to consider the bigger questions of why it is that particular groups of children consistently perform at lower levels than others. An exclusive focus on individual performance must shift to embrace questions of how teachers motivate and inspire particular groups of children while failing to do so with others; how teaching practices most readily enfranchise children whose social/cultural backgrounds mirror most closely the social/cultural mores of the school; how literacy practices in classrooms so often authorize the knowledge, the skills, the desires of particular groups while failing to take account of others; and how constructions of literacy not only privilege a particular classed and cultural subject, but do not take account of the new postmodern literate subject produced through technological and globalised cultural shifts. At its simplest, the question must move from asking what is wrong with the individual child to asking what is wrong with schooling practices that produce such uneven results—in identifiable social demographic patterns—from early periods of school life, and what needs to change in our understanding of "literacy."

The challenge now is to have teachers unpack the assumptions underlying much of what they do in the name of literacy remediation, to think beyond treating the symptoms of failure, and to do the conceptually demanding work necessary in shifting results like those outlined in this article. As we have indicated, work of this kind has already been undertaken in problematising boys' literacy performance within frameworks of gender construction, regulation, and resistance. Similarly, it has been suggested that the low level participation and under-performance of Aboriginal students and Torres Strait Islander students needs to be re-reviewed—rather than as individual failure of the student, as failure of the school to adopt "more culturally-aware and sensitive educational processes" (Reference Group Overseeing the National Review of Education for Aboriginal and Torres Strait Peoples, 1995, p. 15). Teachers need to think beyond integrationist, assimilationist, and culturally imperialist models that attempt to fit everyone into the uncompromising hegemony of the mainstream.

Where the individual child is constantly located as the site of failure, there is little incentive to interrogate mainstream curriculum and schooling practices. Where mainstream curriculum exists as the given, teachers' critical gaze is never reflexively turned on taken-for-granted practices. Failure elicits more of the same. The impetus is to offer individual remediation to assimilate, integrate, and colonise students whose interests do not reflect the interests of the school. It is never quite apparent that it may be the curriculum and teaching practices that are in need of remediation.

In summary, remediation for large numbers of children identifiable by group status, for instance, for boys, for Indigenous and bi-cultural children, and for children from working-class backgrounds, really doesn't seem to make good pedagogic sense. Educators must surely puzzle at how a curriculum centred on literacy learning produces such miserable results in such systematic patterns for so many.

If we as teachers see ourselves in the business of literacy teaching/learning, then perhaps we can stop asking what's wrong with children who don't want what we offer. Instead, we can begin to look at the ways that literacy is produced in the classroom, the ways that it is marketed in the wider community as more appropriate to some groups than others, and the ways that we excite and enthuse sufficient numbers of children not to notice those whom we disenfranchise and disaffect.

The challenge for teachers is two-fold. We must find ways of reading and working with individual performance indicators—and take note of what it is they tell us about what has come to count as literacy at school—while at the same time seeking to contest the versions of literacy and the literate subjects so often enfranchised by such indicators. It seems that we know quite a bit about being under the literacy bench(mark): how do we find ways to get these students out from under?

REFERENCES

Alloway, N. (1995). *Foundation stones: The construction of gender in early childhood.* Carlton, Victoria: Curriculum Corporation.

Alloway, N., & Gilbert, P. (1997). Everything is dangerous: Working with the boys and literacy agenda. *English in Australia, 119/120,* 35–45.

Alloway, N., & Gilbert, P. (Eds). (1997). *Boys and literacy: Professional development units.* Carlton, Victoria: Curriculum Corporation.

Davy, V. (1995). Reaching for consensus on gender equity: The NSW experience. *Proceedings of the Promoting Gender Equity Conference,* 22–24 February. Canberra: Department of Education.

Gilbert, P. (1989). *Writing, schooling and deconstruction: From voice to text in the classroom.* London: Routledge.

Gilbert, P. (1994). *Divided by a common language? Gender and the English curriculum.* Carlton, Victoria: Curriculum Corporation.

Gilbert, R., & Gilbert, P. (in press). *Masculinity goes to school.* Sydney: Allen and Unwin.

Hunter, I. (1988). *Culture and government: The emergence of literary education.* London: Macmillan.

Luke, A. (1992). *When basic skills and information processing just aren't enough: Rethinking reading in new times* (AJA Nelson Address of the 1992 National Conference of the Australian Council for Adult Literacy, pp. 1–24). Townsville, North Queensland, Australia: Australian Councill for Adult Literacy.

Management Committee for the National School English Literacy Survey. (1997). *Mapping literacy achievement.* Canberra: DEETYA.

Martino, W. (1995, February). Gendered learning practices. Exploring the costs of hegemonic masculinity for girls and boys in school. *Proceedings of the Promoting Gender Equity Conference* (pp. 22–24). Canberra: Department of Education.

Masters, G. (1997). *Literacy standards in Australia.* Canberra: DEETYA.

Orlandi, L. (1996). *Children, gender, rurality and written texts.* Unpublished Honours thesis, James Cook University of North Queensland, Townsville.

Patterson, A. (1997). Setting limits to English: Response to Ian Hunter. In S. Muspratt, A. Luke, & P. Freebody (Eds.), *Constructing critical literacies: Teaching and learning textual practice.* Cresskill, NJ: Hampton Press.

Phillips, A. (1993). *The trouble with boys: Parenting the men of the future.* London: Pandora.

Poynton, C. (1985). *Language and gender: Making a difference.* Geelong, Victoria: Deakin University Press.

Reference Group Overseeing the National Review of Education for Aboriginal and Torres Strait Peoples. (1995). *National review of education for Aboriginal and Torres Strait Islander peoples. Final report.* Canberra: DEETYA.

Yunupingu, M. (1994). *National review of education for Aboriginal and Torres Strait Islander peoples: A discussion paper.* Canberra: AGPS.

Assessment, reporting, and accountability in English and literacy education: Finding the signposts to the future

Marion Meiers

Titles for presentations at conferences often seem to be framed in two sections, and this one is no exception. It's not a title with a sub-title— the colon is meant to show that this title is a short piece of writing in two sections. As a piece of writing, it has some interesting features—one is that it's full of nouns!

The first section of this title reflects the strand in this conference to which my presentation is relevant, and thus, I suppose, it indicates the general field to which the discussion belongs. The words in this section resonate with an "official" vocabulary; even more significantly, the first three words are probably representative of some of the currently most contested areas of educational activity. But that's not all—the words "English and literacy education" are intended to set some boundaries, too, but they are also words which generate a multiplicity of responses in listeners and readers.

My intention for the second section of this title is that it should describe the overall purpose of my address—not only to describe the range and variety of the activity which fits under the first section, but to offer some practical suggestions about where we might be headed, hence the use of the only verb, "finding." And there is an intended ambiguity—as educators we need clearly marked signposts for our future work; but those words "assessment, reporting, and accountability" also have major implications for the future lives of our students.

The large scale map and the detailed insert

Signposts have associations with maps, and it's often useful to map the terrain we are travelling through. In this address, I am going to try to identify some of the signposts to future developments on the large scale map

From *Rejoicing in Literacy. Voices of Australia*. The 22nd National Conference of the Australian Literacy Educators' Association, Brisbane Convention and Exhibition Centre, South Bank Brisbane, 30 June–3 July 1996. Reprinted with permission of the Australian Literacy Eduators' Association.

of Australian education which seem to me, late in the 1990s, to hold some importance for us as educators. I also want to look at some of the features of the more detailed map of the landscape of the classroom. This metaphor of a large scale map, accompanied by a more detailed insert, is a useful one in acknowledging how broader issues relating to assessment and reporting, and classroom approaches to assessment and reporting, are intertwined: what we do in the classroom is not separate from the concerns of the wider community.

Different travellers recognise different landmarks; I am going to describe some of the landmarks which are prominent for me. The landmarks I describe have significance for me in relation to the position on assessment and reporting I took, with my co-author, in *Telling the Whole Story* (McGregor & Meiers, 1991).

> Assessment methods should help teachers to focus on what developing speakers, readers, listeners or writers can do, and on what their next steps might be....
>
> Responsive assessment, then, responds to many matters—to the English curriculum, to the social nature of the development of language and thought, to the questions teachers ask, to the varied ways in which students work, to the classroom context, to students' self-assessments, and to what others wish to know about the development and achievement of individual students. Above all, it is responsive to the needs of the individual learner, and the extensive range of evidence students themselves offer about their development and achievement. (McGregor & Meiers, 1991, p. 20)

As I describe the landmarks on my map, you will perhaps be mentally drawing your own maps. The sharing and discussion of our individual maps should lead to some fruitful professional discussion.

The public face of assessment and reporting

What happens in schools, in terms of assessment practices, seems often to become a topic of popular discussion. We are aware of the tendency of the media, from time to time, to publish feature articles decrying "falling standards." However, discussions about assessment and reporting sometimes appear in the public domain in unusual contexts. During January this year, the following strips from the regular comic, *For Better or For Worse*, by Lynn Johnston were featured in the Melbourne *Age*. This series is designed around the realities of everyday life, presenting the quirky nature of events in ways that often move readers to smile, or occasionally, to respond with sympathy to the poignancy of a situation.

In each of these strips we see aspects of curriculum practice and assessment presented for public audiences who, it is assumed, will have the necessary contextual knowledge to appreciate the irony of these situations drawn from real life.

For Better or For Worse®   **by Lynn Johnston**

©Lynn Johnston Productions, Inc./Distributed by United Feature Syndicate, Inc.

This first strip raises the whole question of the purposes of classroom tasks. The question in the final frame highlights the role of students in this enterprise—they often do *not* know why a task is to be completed, and it is important, in the whole teaching and learning cycle, that they *should* have access to the knowledge of the purposes of the work they are required to complete.

For Better or For Worse®   **by Lynn Johnston**

©Lynn Johnston Productions, Inc./Distributed by United Feature Syndicate, Inc.

The second strip appeared subsequently. This time, the dilemma of assessing group work is vividly presented. It's interesting to see the recognition of group work as a common practice. Amongst teachers, there has been much discussion of the issue of how to assess the outcomes of group work when students may contribute unevenly.

For Better or For Worse®   **by Lynn Johnston**

©Lynn Johnston Productions, Inc./Distributed by United Feature Syndicate, Inc.

Three weeks later, the third strip appeared. (The sequence of the comic series seems to mirror life—this is a realistic time frame for the completion of the group task, and for the teacher to have assessed the work.) This pushes the complexity of assessing cooperative ventures a little further, and returns to the question of purposes. This strip, of course, raises another thorny issue—that of the value of marks and grades.

For Better or For Worse®   **by Lynn Johnston**

©Lynn Johnston Productions, Inc./Distributed by United Feature Syndicate, Inc.

The fourth strip rounded off the sequence, reminding us that students often have very different purposes for working in particular ways than the reasons teachers might suppose they have.

The point of considering this sequence is that it exemplifies the ways in which matters of assessment and reporting are relevant to many folk beyond the immediate world of the classroom. This is the aspect of educational practice which perhaps interfaces most directly with the wider community.

The stakeholders

So, we might now ask: "Who are the key players in the whole range of activity broadly represented under the description of 'assessment, reporting, and accountability'?" An initial response is to identify teachers as being highly significant players, and to assert the validity of the professional judgment of teachers. But there are other stakeholders, too, whose voices are heard in the discussion: the State (politicians, policy makers, and bureaucrats), the media, parents, employers.

In the past decade we have seen a heightened awareness within the teaching profession, and the wider community, of the complex lines of accountability involved in the assessment and reporting of students' learning outcomes. This has been particularly so in relation to English and literacy education, in contexts such as the introduction of basic skills testing, or in media reports about the relationships between literacy standards and teaching practices.

Around Australia, it's very clear that contemporary educational decision making and planning involves complex interactions between the teaching profession, and policy makers and politicians. There is no doubt that there is a political aspect involved in the broad shaping of curriculum. We've seen how recent changes of government have initiated processes of curriculum review and change, for example in the 1995 Eltis review which followed the election of the NSW Labour government.

There is no doubt about the legitimacy of the interest of the State in the goals, standards, and outcomes of schooling and the curriculum. This stems from the State's responsibility in democratic societies for the provision of comprehensive and equitable educational opportunities for all children, and increasingly, for life-long educational opportunities for all people in society. The State's role is to ensure access to education for all, and to maintain the quality of educational provision.

Furthermore, the State, as the key provider of funding for schooling, undoubtedly has a legitimate interest in the efficiency and effectiveness with which that funding is being used. This means that the State will become involved in the scope and nature of literacy and English curriculum provision, and in the standards (or outcomes) achieved by students working within that curriculum.

Some current developments

Let us take this exploration of who's who in assessment and reporting a little further by looking at some developments in the current context which seemingly have implications for what might occur in classrooms—the landmarks on the large scale map.

1. From the public sector

My first example comes from the public sector. The first *Report on Government Service Provision* from the Steering Committee for the Review of Commonwealth/ State Service Provision was published in 1995. Under the auspices of COAG— the Council of Australian Governments—this report presents information relating to the effectiveness and efficiency of a number of government-funded services, including education.

The report draws attention to the perceived importance of monitoring the performance of government services.

> Governments play a lead role in funding, providing and regulating social infrastructure services such as health and community services, education and training, and justice. As these services are integral to the quality of life in Australia, how well they are delivered is important to us all.
>
> Any assessment of performance must include consideration of both efficiency and effectiveness. The effectiveness of these services in achieving the desired policy outcomes set by governments is important. It is also important that these services are provided efficiently given the large share of the nation's resources employed in these sectors and the major impact they have on our overall economic performance.
>
> Performance monitoring is one of a number of ways of ensuring incentives are in place for government provided services to achieve desired outcomes and over time, raise performance levels. (Steering Committee for the Review of Commonwealth/State Service Provision, 1995, p. iii)

The section of the report which deals with Government School Education describes how the effectiveness indicators which address the range of objectives pursued at the system level are generally based on the Common and Agreed National Goals for Schooling in Australia (Australian Education Council, 1989). The report refers to student learning outcomes, social and other, and equity objectives. The efficiency objectives focus on costs per student.

What data does the report draw on in relation to student learning outcomes? The need for action to address the lack of nationally comparable data is noted.

> It is anticipated that the National School English Literacy Survey, to be completed by the end of 1996, will go some way to addressing the lack of comparable outcomes data, and will provide important information in terms of literacy. (Steering Committee for the Review of Commonwealth/ State Service Provision, 1995, p. 200)

(More of this Survey later.)

The report describes the two main ways in which student learning outcomes are assessed, beginning by acknowledging what teachers do:

> Student learning outcomes are assessed by teachers in classrooms on an ongoing basis. In addition, standard testing instruments are used to supplement this information. Standard tests are particularly suited to system-wide assessments of student learning outcomes. Unlike teacher assessments their statistical validity is not affected by the unknown differences in the way teachers across the system approach the task of assessment.

The limitations of standard tests are acknowledged:

> Standard tests, however, are not without limitations. As a basis for making comparisons, either over time or between systems at one point in time, they are limited by varying results due to varying efforts by teachers to "teach to the test" rather than the wider curriculum; the inability of standard tests to cater to the different cultural or ethnic backgrounds of students; and, in some cases, the limited range of earning outcomes addressed. In addition, tests may not be able to measure performance in all the broader constructs of a particular learning area.

However, the report seems to look towards a way of addressing these limitations:

> Some of these problems are being addressed to some extent through the development by the school systems of more sophisticated standard assessments, including the incorporation of assessments based on portfolios of student work. (Steering Committee for the Review of Commonwealth/State Service Provision, 1995, p. 213)

The implications of this report, and of the annual reports which will follow it, merit serious consideration, especially in relation to professional views about standard tests.

2. Articulating parents' viewpoints

Parent organisations, too, have recently articulated clear views in relation to assessment and reporting. They see themselves as "active partners in the education enterprise" (Australian Council of State School Organisations [ACSSO] & Australian Parents Council [APC], 1996). In the *Report of the Assessment and Reporting for Parents Project*, the perspective of parents is stated thus:

Parents believe that quality school education is the entitlement of every young Australian. Parents also believe that the school curriculum should be designed to enrich their children's lives and help prepare them to participate fully in society and the workplace.

Assessment and reporting should be integral to the curriculum that students follow and should not narrow or distort the experience of schooling. An appropriate, well thought out school curriculum should encompass equally appropriate and well thought out assessment procedures. The latter should not drive the former. (ACSSO & APC, 1996, p. 3).

Here, the emphasis is on the place of assessment and reporting in the whole teaching and learning cycle. The principle of two-way communication is stated clearly:

Sustained two-way communication about progress and the improvement of learning is vital throughout the school years. It should be grounded in carefully collected and interpreted information. Assessment is the process of gathering information about student learning, especially in relation to curriculum goals. Reporting should relay information in ways which are supported, accessible and meaningful to parents and students. Analysing information, making judgments and developing plans for future learning are ongoing outcomes of these activities. The most powerful results occur when parents, students and teachers actively participate in all facets of these processes. (ACSSO & APC, 1996, p. 3)

Embedded in this statement we find a clear definition: "Assessment is the process of gathering information about student learning, especially in relation to curriculum goals." The active partnership between parents, students, and teachers is emphasised. The focus is on "progress and the improvement of learning." As in the COAG report, the connections between assessment information and curriculum goals are noted.

The perspective on the provision of data at the system level is different from the perspective of the COAG report, but nevertheless, recognises the legitimacy of governments' interest:

A second purpose for assessment and reporting is to respond to increasing pressure from State and Commonwealth Governments to make available data to inform policy considerations about the effectiveness of schools and schooling. Any requirement for the provision of such data must be consistent with the educational role of schools, and must maintain student confidence and contribute to the achievement of social justice and equity. (ACSSO & APC, 1996, p. 4)

Here we see a focus on "effectiveness," linked to social justice and equity.

This report argues a case for the improvement of the processes of assessment and reporting. It outlines the changing context for schooling, focusing on social and cultural exchange, labour market change, technological change, and on the change to an "outcomes" approach. The increasing concern with outcomes, and the influence on curriculum design, implementation and assessment, and reporting processes is described. Two viewpoints on outcomes are presented:

> On the one hand, "outcomes" as descriptions of intended and actual learning can help recognition of achievement and where this fits on an individual learning continuum. "Outcomes" can be an important element in teachers working together to make judgments about achievement and the teaching necessary to facilitate future learning. Their implementation can lead to procedures which reflect the integrity of the curriculum, enhance student engagement and help parents to remain informed about children's progress.
>
> On the other hand, the "outcomes" approach can lead to the breaking down of complex learnings into a myriad of disconnected parts, all of which require assessing. When this form of "outcomes" is injected into statewide curriculum syllabuses, significance is lost, over-assessing occurs, and teaching is prescribed rather than informed by the child's needs and the teacher's experience. Further tensions are created when this form of "outcomes" is aggregated into standardised device against which achievement is measured. (ACSSO & APC, 1996, p. 4)

This very effectively captures the paradoxical nature of "outcomes"—stressing the value of individual learning continua, but warning of potential dangers.

The views in the parent associations' report match those presented in the Australian Literacy Federation's position paper on assessment and reporting. The ALF paper is intended to provide a general position on assessment and reporting which might inform more specific work within the five ALF associations. The opening paragraphs of the paper read as follows:

> Assessment is the process of collecting a range of information about learners and their diverse achievements, and about performance, and making judgments about the significance of this information. Reporting is the process of communicating the results of the assessment to the stakeholders in appropriate forms.
>
> Assessment and reporting of development and achievement in English language and literacy must acknowledge the complexity of learning in general and learning language in particular. It needs to consider the diverse nature of learners.... (Australian Literacy Federation, 1995)

Notice the similarity between this definition of what assessment is, and the definition in the report from the parent associations. So, here's another landmark on the map—that which represents the articulated perspectives of parents.

3. Outcomes based education

There isn't time here to trace the evolution of outcomes approaches during this decade, but this is, of course, another significant "landmark" on the map. As both the COAG report, and the parent report recognise, the "outcomes" approach is an important contextual influence.

Outcomes are integral to the national statements and profiles, and it's useful to note that we do have at least two guides to the ways in which these documents developed through the national collaborative curriculum work from 1989 to 1993. Helen Campagna-Wildash's article, intriguingly titled, "For the record: an anonymous hack comes out" in the *Australian Journal of Language and Literacy*, June 1995, narrates her experiences as a key writer of the English Statement and Profile. Another important background article is that written by Richard Jenkin for the Children's Literacy Research project jointly conducted by Dilena and van Krayenoord, "Whole School Approaches to Assessing and Reporting Literacy." Jenkin's article is entitled "Australian national collaborative curriculum development—a tangled web" (Jenkin, 1996).

> Like politics, curriculum is the art of the possible. The published documents are a consequence of bargaining, compromises and deals. In the end, however, the products must stand the acid test—can teachers use the statements and profiles to assist them in improving the learning outcomes of all students? (Jenkin, 1996, p. 17)

This is, indeed, the acid test, and a question which we must keep asking ourselves. It is too early to be able to answer the question. As I wrote in the editorial to the June 1995 edition of the *Australian Journal of Language and Literacy*,

> It is too early to tell the whole story of the impact of the statements and profiles on Australian education. Indeed, there may never be a point when it is possible to tell that story. (Meiers, 1995)

But the impact of these initiatives, and of the ongoing implementation of outcomes approaches, is most definitely one of those important features of the current educational map. As the states and territories develop their own versions of the nationally developed documents, we are already seeing interesting diversity, according to the differing educational contexts in each state and territory.

In Western Australia, the development of an additional "Viewing" strand will be a great interest. Victorian teachers are this year addressing the need to include information on students' achievement according to the levels and strands of the Curriculum and Standards Framework in school annual reports, and in reports to parents. This task raises a multiplicity of issues: the kind of assessment information needed; record keeping; reliability; the differences between levels of performance of particular pieces of work; and the kind of overall achievement which can be represented with the CSF.

Sharing the knowledge which will accrue during this period of implementation will provide us with some of the answers, and is also likely to suggest further questions.

4. Progress maps

The ARK materials—Assessment Resource Kit—developed by Forster and Masters provide us with yet another perspective on outcomes—a perspective they describe as "developmental assessment"!

> Developmental assessment shifts the focus in assessment from notions of "passing" and "failing" to the concept of ongoing growth: from an emphasis on comparing one individual with another to an emphasis on students' developing skills, knowledge and understandings.
>
> Developmental assessment provides a broader perspective on student growth than is available in a single classroom. A progress map draws on experience and evidence from a wide range of classrooms. It also sets student growth in the context of growth made in earlier years of school and progress that can reasonably be expected in the future. In other words, a progress map provides a "whole school" view of teaming. (Masters and Forster, 1996, p. 8)

There are currently many examples of progress maps in use in Australia. The well-known First Steps developmental continua is one example; the profiles for Australian schools is another. The definition of outcomes provided in the profiles reads:

> Outcomes describe in progressive order the various skills and knowledge that students typically acquire as they become proficient in any area. They are the building blocks of the profile. (Curriculum Corporation, 1994, p. 5)

The increasing use of progress maps is, then, another landmark to plot on the map.

5. A National School English Literacy Survey

The National School English Literacy Survey, which will take place from August 12 in all Australian states and territories, has been designed to collect nationally comparable data on students' literacy achievement at Years 3 and 5. This data will provide benchmark information for a range of purposes.

The methodology for the Survey has a number of significant aspects. Firstly, it is based on the strands and levels of the English Curriculum Profile for Australian Schools. This provides the basis for gathering data to build a rich picture of literacy—of reading, viewing, and writing integrated with speaking and listening.

Secondly, the Survey will collect two sets of data from a voluntary, representative national sample of 4,500 students at each year level, including over-sampling for an Aboriginal sample, including urban, rural, and remote communities. A set of school, teacher, and student questionnaires will collect information on background variables, such as gender, socio-economic status, and non-English speaking background. This information will be used in association with portfolios of students' responses to common assessment tasks in speaking, listening, reading, viewing, and writing, and examples of students' best work in speaking and writing. The use of centrally designed assessment tasks, marking guides, and criteria provides the basis for reliability.

The third significant aspect is the centrality of teacher judgment. Teachers will work in association with trained external assessors to assess their own students' work, using the common marking guides and criteria. The professional development and training of both the external assessors, and the participating teachers is designed to support reliability and comparability.

This methodology is extremely interesting, and breaks new ground. A spin-off is likely to be in the way the common tasks may well provide examples of assessment tasks which teachers can use as models in their own classrooms.

This survey is another current development which seems to be emerging as a landmark activity in Australian education.

Meantime, in the classroom...

Ultimately, the classroom is the site where the impact of the influence of the range of current developments becomes most visible. Within the classroom, teachers are positioned to constantly monitor and respond to the varied development and achievement of their students.

But teachers also look outward from their classrooms to acknowledge the interests of other stakeholders. State endorsed curriculum documents like the Queensland English syllabus, the English statement and profile in South Australia, or the Victorian Curriculum and Standards Framework, set the broad parameters for what is taught, and represent the state's role. Home school partnerships often operate very effectively to ensure that parents and caregivers contribute to their child's education. Schools issue regular reports to parents on students' progress, in one of the most critical lines of communication between home and school.

But what are we really talking about when we describe how these links between three of the key stakeholder groups actually work in practice? We certainly hear, from each group, many questions—and various answers to these questions. What counts as evidence of achievement? How can we appropriately describe development in something as complex and multi-faceted as competence in literacy and English? What benchmarks and criteria can we reliably and validly use to describe achievement? Why has there been an increase in the incidence of basic skills testing for whole cohorts of students? What is the nature of the links between curriculum planning, assessment, and reporting? Who are those parties with legitimate interests in student learning outcomes? Do different stakeholders require different kinds of information? What recent developments in teaching practice are helping to provide valid and reliable assessment information? How might such information be used?

This list of questions suggests the multiplicity of issues involved in any discussion relating to assessment and reporting. It is clear that there are no simple answers.

A series of scenarios, in which activities relating to assessment and reporting are enacted in the context of the classroom, might highlight some answers to these and other questions.

Scenario one: Students at work

Within the setting of the classroom, a small group discussion is in progress. The teacher has taken the opportunity to observe students at work, to gather some useful assessment information by taking some brief notes on two or three students, and to provide feedback to different students as they participate in the activity. The teacher has carefully planned this activity so that it will create opportunities for students to achieve a variety of learning goals.

Such planning opens up the possibility of gathering the wide range of evidence implied in Eisner's view that we need assessment information drawn from a wide variety of contexts:

> ...simply knowing the final score of the game after it is over is not very useful. What we need is a vivid rendering of how that game is being played.... (Eisner, 1980)

The planning for this activity took account of a wide range of learning outcomes, and of the previous experiences of the class. The teachers' knowledge of one of the maps of progress referred to earlier provides a focus for observing particular aspects of the students' work.

Let's identify some key aspects of this scenario, and try to match them with the directions on the large scale map.

Key aspects:

• planning

• a variety of assessment information

• reference to a map of progress

Scenario two: Responding to a piece of writing

It's morning recess: student stops a teacher (who happens to be on yard duty) in the corridor: "Have you read my piece of writing yet?"

What might the teacher say to this student? The student seems eager to hear some suggestions about what to do next, and is enthusiastic about the writing task. What questions need to be considered before an appropriate answer is given? In any situation like this, there are actually many questions to be considered. Here is the list I generated when writing an account of how we might respond to one student's writing:

• What was the activity within which this writing was generated? What were the requirements of the task?

• Is this a draft or a finished piece of writing?

• What advice might assist this student to further develop this draft, if it is a draft?

• If this is a finished piece, what suggestions might be made about what the student should do next, in terms of developing further competence in writing?

• What does this piece of writing indicate about what this student can do, as far as writing is concerned?

• As a piece of writing, how effective is this work?

• Does this piece of writing show evidence of other aspects of English— reading and response to texts, speaking and listening, the exploration of challenging ideas and issues?

• What are the differences between responding to a single piece of writing, and to a collection of writing in a portfolio?

- What explicit assessment criteria might be used to appraise the work? Should these criteria be related to the writing task, or to generic features of writing?

When I considered this list, I realised that:

All of these questions are actually relevant to any occasion involving teachers in responding to students' writing. When posed as a set of questions, as has been done here, the close connections between planning and assessment are highlighted, as is the necessity of attending to the whole teaching and learning context when responding to students' writing.

The context within which any piece of writing is generated and develops is always an important influence in shaping the teacher's response: there are many differences between appropriate responses to journal writing, for example, and to a developing short story,... If a particular task has been set, there will be different parameters to the teacher's response than if a piece of "free writing" is under consideration. The stage at which the writer seeks a response strongly determines the kinds of feedback which will support developing writers: feedback on a draft will suggest possibilities for experimenting, for re-shaping the structure, for attending to matters of style and conventions; feedback on finished work can appropriately explore the scope of what has been achieved, and what might be done next. (Meiers, 1996)

Key aspects:

- connections between planning and assessment

- responses relevant to different stages of the teaching and learning cycle

- focus on "what next?"

- an opportunity to provide the "vivid rendering of how that game is being played"

Scenario three: Exploring work samples

In the 1995 NPDP project conducted by the Australian Literacy Federation in association with the Curriculum Corporation, teachers from around Australia provided samples of their own students' work which they had annotated against the strands and levels of the English profile. Many of them consulted with colleagues in developing these annotations; an ALF expert reference group moderated the whole collection in order to provide a set of comparable work samples which could assist teachers in making reliable judgments about their own students' work.

The process used to annotate the work samples in this collection suggests a model for teachers assessing their own students' work, when it might be necessary to report judgements of achievement against the levels and strands of the English profile. There are a number of clear stages in the sequence of annotating work:

- Read/observe/listen to/view the sample of student work.
- Describe the achievement shown in the work ("This work sample indicates that this student can....").
- Label each item on this list according to the strand and strand organiser it most closely fits within. For example, "Can write a simple narrative" would fit within Writing: Texts. "Can listen and respond to peers in problem-solving groups" would fit within Speaking and Listening: Texts.
- Make an on-balance judgement about the level of achievement within the relevant strands and strand organizers.
- Write a summary comment which describes the levels of achievement indicated by the sample of work, "This work is indicative of achievement of the following outcomes...." (Australian Literacy Federation, forthcoming, introduction)

Even though the samples in this collection often include more than one piece of work from one student, this is not intended to suggest that it is appropriate to make judgments of overall achievement on the basis of a limited range of work. For this reason, the phrase *This work is indicative of achievement of the following outcomes* is used throughout the collection, as a constant reminder of the importance of basing judgements about outcomes achieved and levels of achievement on evidence of a wide range of work, collected over significant periods of time, such as a semester or year.

Sets of annotated work samples can be used by teachers as a record of an individual student's development, and as a reference point for continuing assessment.

Teachers always know far more about a student's development and achievement than can be seen in a single set of work samples, and, in practice, this professional knowledge plays a vital role in assessment. There are many details which can be described in annotating work samples, and, in the ALF collection, no attempt was made to say everything which might be said about a particular sample. Rather, the annotations refer to key features relevant to the aspect of English curriculum which is the focus of each main section.

In assessing achievement in terms of the levels and outcomes of the Profile, as a map of progress, it is always important to consider the nature of the activity which prompted the work. In the ALF collection, the background to each activity has been described in some detail for each work sample.

Key aspects:
- teachers' work in selecting and annotating a collection of work samples
- basing judgments on a wide range of evidence
- providing support for comparability of judgments

Scenario four: Using assessment criteria

The three scenarios above describe situations where the prime purpose of making an assessment is formative, where the emphasis is on monitoring development, on responding to work with the intention of making suggestions about what to do next. There are other occasions when it is appropriate to make a summative assessment of particular examples of work.

The school assessed Common Assessment Tasks (CATs) for the common, compulsory VCE English study in Victoria—a high stakes assessment context—comprise fifty percent of the final assessment in the subject. Teachers assess their own students' work, using centrally defined criteria. For reliability purposes, a sample of work from across the state is reviewed by trained reviewers using the same set of criteria. Thus, the assessment process in this case is classroom based, and constructed around the use of criteria.

The second Common Assessment Task is a writing folio, made up of a selection of three pieces of finished writing, each written for a different purpose.

The set of either centrally prescribed criteria is grouped into four clusters:

Thought and content (the quality of thinking and knowledge demonstrated in the work)
1. knowledge and control of the chosen content
2. effectiveness and appropriateness of the exploration of ideas and issues

Structure and organisation
3. coherence and development of ideas and information
4. effectiveness of the structure developed in response to the specific task

Expression, style, and mechanics
5. expressiveness and fluency
6. effectiveness and appropriateness of the language chosen
7. control of the mechanics of the English language to support meaning

Appropriate variation of content, structure, and language for different purposes and audiences

8. capacity to select the most effective means of communicating meaning, given the intended audiences and purposes.

Let's look at the opening sentences of each piece in one folio in order to gain a sense of the quality and flavour of the writing:

Piece 1

The tram arrives at the St Kilda terminal, preparing to commence the long journey to Kew. The bleak, grey morning clouds the city in a deep fog. only a few board the tram here.

At this time of morning, the streets still lie relatively still lie undisturbed, but after crossing St Kilda Road, the surroundings seem to come to life. From the vantage point of the tram window, one gains an insight into the lives of Carlisle Street dwellers.

Piece 2

Important memo to all year twelve students regarding last week's formal:

As you all well know, the year 12 formal allowed you a fun time with your friends and a night to forget about study. as one of the most important social functions of your final year of school, I hope you all thoroughly enjoyed it. For many of you it may have been your first formal, and thus you were unable to rate the night as you didn't know what to expect. To assist you in evaluating your personal enjoyment of the night, I have provided some assessment criteria below....

Piece 3

The aroma. Pine-O-Clean mixed with the overpowering stench of TV dinners, this is what I first notice. as my nose becomes accustomed to the smell, my eyes fall upon the surroundings. It is a sight I have seen many times, yet one which always alarms me. Whitewashed walls. Grey floors. Tacky furniture. And all around, wheelchairs and walking aids with absent faces peering out from under them. yet this is not a hospital. it is my grandmother's 'home.' mum and I slowly make our way up the stairs. Our shoes squeak on the linoleum floor, announcing our arrival to the nurses on duty.

She is sitting in the corner of the room.... (Board of Studies, 1996)

This is a very successful folio, at the top of the "A" range, but not quite an A+. The three pieces have been very well selected to provide evidence of this writer's flexibility and versatility. The tone, style, and form of each piece are markedly different.

The statements of intention for each piece describe the development of each piece, indicating the various decisions the writer has made to accommodate the demands of audience and purpose. Where the original intention for writing has been changed in the process of writing, or the tone has developed as the piece progressed, this has been described. The work itself reflects this understanding of the interplay between audience and purpose and a wide range of aspects of writing.

The writer has successfully used two very different models for the first two pieces. The first piece builds on a reading of *Journeyings* (Janet McCalman, Melbourne University Press, 1993), exploring some issues relating to schooling and social diversity. In using the VCE English criteria as a model for the second piece, the writer has shown a strong understanding of a way of appealing to the target audience. The bringing together of two major aspects of the life of year 12 students—CATs and the "formal"— is a strategic move in developing a humorous piece. The third piece explores personal experience to convey a significant range of emotion.

The whole folio strongly reflects the writer's capacity to vary content, structure, and language for different purposes and audiences. The writing is fluent and expressive, and across the three pieces shows a well-developed capacity to choose vocabulary, tone, and style appropriate to the particular context of the piece.

In relation to the criteria relating to thought and content, the folio shows impressive knowledge and control of the chosen content. In each piece, the content is of significance, and this significance is successfully communicated to the reader. Each piece is carefully focused, and content has been selected to emphasise particular impressions. There is evidence of exploration of some of the implications and complexities of the ideas and issues underlying each of the three pieces. It is interesting to note the different approaches—one through a description focusing on selected details, the second through descriptive detail shaped by the nature of CAT assessment criteria, and the third piece in a narrative style.

Structure has been carefully considered, and a variety of overall structures offered. The first piece uses the journey itself to provide a structure, the second uses the framework of the criteria, while the third piece uses the chronology of the actual visit to provide sequence and coherence within the piece.

Key aspects:
- assessing a collection of work
- using criteria to describe achievement
- summative judgments

Scenario five: Designing a school report format

A group of teachers is meeting (after school), to take up the directions of the school's revised assessment and reporting policy. Their brief is to review and possibly to suggest some revisions to the report format used by the school over the past three years.

The conversation moves around central questions such as:

"We'll need to keep the section that summarises the curriculum and assessment program for each class, won't we?"

"Yes, but it will need to be up-dated, I think."

"Where will we include information on the students' achievement in relation to the profile levels?"

"That's going to need a new section."

"Anyway, we can do that at the same time as we get that information ready for the school annual report, can't we?"

"Oh, and that's going to mean we have to meet in year level groups to work out how we're going to decide on these levels—we'll have to be consistent. Maybe we could use some work samples...."

"This report form leaves space for a lot of information about the students' strengths, and those things which need extra support."

"Well, that definitely must stay—it's probably the most important thing."

"Do we have enough space for some comment on things like attitude, participation, and social skills—you know, our parents have always seemed to like that."

"Are we still going to give grades?"

"What about students' self assessments?"

"Mm...we'll need to think about that."

"We should be able to use the computer to design this format, and to help with entering information."

"Yes, but it's really important that we keep a sense of each individual child...."

"You know, we're really saying that we can keep a lot of the current format—we're talking about revisions...."

And so the work would continue. These conversations are happening in many places at present, and in many ways, they bring together key elements in the whole discussion of assessment and reporting, perhaps because they represent the interface between the classroom and the wider community.

Key aspects:

• inclusion of information about the curriculum and assessment program

• information about levels

• reporting on individual strengths and areas needing support

The quality of assessment information

If we collate the lists of key features identified for each of these scenarios, we might be able to recognise some of the "signposts" I mentioned at the beginning.

• planning
• a variety of assessment information
• reference to a map of progress

• connections between planning and assessment
• responses relevant to different stages of the teaching and learning cycle
• focus on "what next?"
• an opportunity to provide the "Vivid rendering of how that game is being played"

• teachers' work in selecting and annotating a collection of work samples
• basing judgements on a wide range of evidence
• providing support for comparability of judgments

• assessing a collection of work
• using criteria to describe achievement
• summative judgements

• inclusion of information about the curriculum and assessment program
• information about levels
• reporting on individual strengths and areas needing support

This really is a list of some of the major issues we need to work with. Comparability of assessments; the range of assessment information; the use of maps of progress and assessment criteria; appropriate reporting formats. There is a consistency between these concerns, and the concerns that could be recognised on the large scale map.

The scenarios described above remind us of how assessment information comes in many guises: formative, summative, reported and unreported, comparative. Sometimes it is derived from direct experience and observation of students in the classroom, and from evidence of their work over extended periods of time; at other times it comes from tests, including specially designed standardised tests. Overall, it is generally agreed that assessment information must be responsive to and reflect the teaching and learning in the classroom. Partial assessments of teaching and learning lack credibility and can lead to the making of inappropriate decisions based on insufficient and unbalanced information.

At the centre of all of these considerations is the quality of the teaching and learning programs we offer, the opportunities we create to gather a rich and diverse range of assessment information, and our professional capacity to interpret that information.

The quality of all assessment information, from the formative, ongoing assessment within the ebb and flow of classroom life, to the information on student outcomes valued in the public sector, depends entirely on the quality of what happens in classrooms. This affirms the significance of teacher judgment in assessing development and achievement. Unless we get this right the whole array of other information will clearly be quite inadequate. The signpost points very clearly in the direction of the classroom.

REFERENCES

Australian Council of State School Organisations & Australian Parents Council. (1996). *Report of the Assessment and Reporting for Parents Project*.

Australian Education Council. (1989). *The Hobart declaration on schooling*. Melbourne, Australia: Author.

Australian Literacy Federation. (1995, November). Assessment and reporting in English language and literacy. *Common Ground, 3*.

Australian Literacy Federation. (1996). *English work samples*. Carlton (in press): Curriculum Corporation.

Board of Studies. (1996). *Official sample CATs 1996, VCE English*. Carlton: Author.

Campagna-Wildash, H. (1995). For the record—an anonymous hack comes out. *Australian Journal of Language and Literacy, 18(2)*.

Curriculum Corporation. (1994). *English—A curriculum profile for Australian schools*. Carlton, Australia: Author.

Eisner, E.W. (1980, Autumn). The impoverished mind. *Curriculum, 1(2)*.

Forster, M. & Masters, G. (1996). *Portfolios: Assessment resource kit*. Camberwell: Australian Council for Educational Research.

Jenkin, R. (1996). Australian national collaborative curriculum development—a tangled web. In Dilena, M. & van Krayenoord, C., *Whole school approaches to assessing and reporting literacy: Final report* (Children's Literacy Project).

Masters, G. & Forster, M. (1996). *Developmental assessment: Assessment resource kit*. Camberwell: Australian Council for Educational Research.

McGregor, R. & Meiers, M. (1991). *Telling the whole story: Assessing achievement in English.* Camberwell: Australian Council for Educational Research.

Meiers, M. (1994). *Exploring the English curriculum statement and profile for Australian schools.* Carlton: Australian Literacy Federation.

Meiers, M. (1995). The English curriculum statement and profile for Australian schools: Tuning in to a national conversation. *Australian Journal of Language and Literacy, 18*(2).

Meiers, M. (1996). The CSF and the VCE: Frameworks for responding to students' writing. *Idiom 1: Responding to students' writing.* Melbourne: VATE.

Steering Committee for the Review of Commonwealth/State Service Provision. (1995). *Report on government service provision.* Melbourne: Author.